BUDDHISM

IN INDIA, CEYLON, CHINA AND JAPAN

BUDDHISM

IN INDIA, CEYLON, CHINA AND JAPAN

A Reading Guide

ARNOLD LUPTON

GYAN

Published by

Gyan Publishing House
5, Ansari Road
Daryaganj, New Delhi-110002
Phone: 011-47034999, 9811692060
E-mail: books@gyanbooks.com

Distribution Network
gyanbooks.com
India, USA, Canada, UK, Australia

ISBN: 978-93-6780-280-9 (HB)

First Published, 1931

2nd Impression 2024

Printed at: Gyan Press, Delhi.

BUDDHISM IN INDIA, CEYLON, CHINA AND JAPAN: A READING GUIDE

Author: CLARENCE H. HAMILTON

BUDDHISM IN INDIA, CEYLON CHINA AND JAPAN

BUDDHISM
IN INDIA, CEYLON, CHINA AND JAPAN

A Reading Guide

BY CLARENCE H. HAMILTON, PH.D.

Professor of Eastern Philosophy in the College of Missions at Hartford Seminary Foundation; Professor of Philosophy in the University of Nanking, China, 1914–27; Visiting Lecturer on Oriental Religions at Columbia University of the City of New York in the Winter of 1927

THE UNIVERSITY OF CHICAGO PRESS
CHICAGO · ILLINOIS

FOREWORD

The rapid growth of relationships between Orient and Occident today presses increasingly upon thoughtful persons in each hemisphere the task of knowing the cultural memories of each other's groups. To aid in this task, especially from the Western side, this brief guide to readings in Buddhism has been prepared.

Buddhism is a cultural phenomenon of immense importance in the experience of Asia. Its study is significant for many kinds of understanding—psychological, social, and religious. But the literature is enormous in scope, reflecting conditions of many different countries in diverse periods of historical change. The beginner is not infrequently discouraged because he cannot see the wood for the trees, while resort to brief treatises too often leaves an impression that is either shallow or unintelligible. The effort here has been to present the subject for four of the great Buddhist countries in a form compact enough to maintain the large outlines of its development and at the same time make clear its vast range and depth. As an instrument of study it should enable the beginner to find his way forward more rapidly and intelligently.

It is assumed that the reader will want to work some topics more intensively than others. For this purpose the special references are given. The outlines are added simply to afford general orientation in adjacent topics. To avoid misunderstanding it should, perhaps, be added that there is nothing final about the outlines, and that the Bibliography, while reasonably full, does not aim to be exhaustive. A full measure of the joys of discovery is left to the reader himself.

For personal encouragement and suggestion the writer is indebted to Professors Robert Ernest Hume, of Union Theological Seminary; Lewis Hodous, of Hartford Seminary Foundation; Kenneth J. Saunders, of the Pacific School of Religion; and A. Eustace Haydon, of the University of Chicago. For friendly co-operation of the professors teaching the religion courses in Columbia University a word of special appreciation is due. It was their interest that suggested a work of this character, and it was for their use that the original draft of these pages was first prepared.

CLARENCE H. HAMILTON

HARTFORD, CONN.
January, 1931

CONTENTS

PART I

IN INDIA: EMERGENCE AND REABSORPTION

I. The Social and Intellectual Background of Early Buddhism

a) References

Davids, T. W. Rhys: *Buddhism: Its History and Literature*, Lecture I.

Davids, T. W. Rhys: *Buddhist India.* (A standard reference. See chaps. i–vi for political and economic conditions; and chaps. xii–xiii for the religious conditions.)

Davids, T. W. Rhys: The Early History of the Buddhists. In the *Cambridge History of India*, I, 171–97. (Briefer presentation of materials of second reference.)

Davids, Mrs. C. A. F. Rhys: "Economic Conditions according to Early Buddhist Literature," *Cambridge History of India*, I, 198–219. (An analysis of the early literature with reference to economic, commercial, social, etc., activities.)

Eliot, Sir Charles: *Hinduism and Buddhism*, I, 87–104. (By one of the most comprehensive students of Buddhism.)

Farquhar, J. N.: *An Outline of the Religious Literature of India*, chap. ii. (Illuminating statement of the religious problem.)

Smith, V. A.: *Oxford Student's History of India*, chap. iii. (Good brief account of early Hindu civilization.)

b) Outline: characteristics of the age in which Buddha lived

1. Simplicity of life in political, economic, and social phases
2. Great intellectual activity, springing in part from
   (*a*) The leisure afforded by the tranquil village life
   (*b*) The native speculative interest of the Hindu mind
3. General acceptance of notions of transmigration and *karma*

4. The presence of wandering, ascetic teachers, claiming to have found the way of escape from endless births and deaths
5. The currency of many disciplines of deliverance
   (*a*) Brahmanic—salvation through realizing the oneness of Brahma and Atman
   (*b*) Lokayatas—salvation through a materialistic philosophy
   (*c*) Jain—salvation through asceticism and non-injury
   (*d*) "Sixty-two heresies," listed in the Brahma Jala Sutta (see Davids, *Buddhism*, chap. ii).
      (1) On the eternity of the world
      (2) Whether souls are eternal or not
      (3) Whether the world is finite, infinite, both, or neither
      (4) On virtue and vice
      (5) On the origin of things without a cause
      (6) On the future existence of souls
      (7) On the destruction of the soul at the end of either this, the next, or subsequent lives
      (8) On the belief that there is a soul and that it can attain to perfect bliss in the present world, or wherever it happens to be

Note the social position enjoyed by the ascetic religious teacher (see reference to Eliot above).

II. The Life of Buddha

a) References

Davids, T. W. Rhys: *Buddhism: Its History and Literature*, pp. 87–117. (A classic sketch by an authority.)

Davids, T. W. Rhys: *Buddhism, Being a Sketch of the Life and Teachings of Gautama, the Buddha* (1877; rev. ed., 1914)

Eliot, Sir Charles: *Hinduism and Buddhism*, I, 129–84.

Geden, A. S.: Article on Buddha in *Encyclopedia of Religion and Ethics* (*ERE*), Vol. II.

Oldenberg, Hermann: *Buddha: Sein Leben, seine Lehre,*

seine Gemeinde (1881). (Still a standard work. English translation by Hoey, in 1882.)

Pratt, J. B.: *The Pilgrimage of Buddhism*, chap. i. (An analysis of Buddha's personality.)

Saunders, Kenneth J.: *Gotama Buddha.* (Based on the canonical books of the Theravadin. An attractive and appreciative treatment by one long acquainted with "southern" Buddhism.)

Thomas, E. J.: *The Life of Buddha as Legend and History* (1927). (The latest critical study, utilizing both Pali and Sanskrit sources.)

SOURCE MATERIALS

Abhinishkramana Sutra. (Elaborately legendary; see below, p. 5.)

Bigandet, P.: *Life or Legend of Gaudama, the Buddha of the Burmese.* (A late work, two thousand years after Buddha.)

Brewster, E. H.: *The Life of Gotama the Buddha* (1926). (Compiled exclusively from the Pali canon. Excellent presentation of all the biographical materials in the Pali texts.)

Buddha-Carita, "Sacred Books of the East," SBE, Vol. XLIX. (See below, p. 5.)

Fo-sho-hing-tsan-king, ibid., Vol. XIX. (A Chinese version of *Buddha-Carita.*)

Jatakas, or Stories of the Buddha's Former Births. 6 vols. Cambridge, 1895–1907.

Krom, N. J.: *The Life of Buddha on the Stupa of Barabudur according to the Lalitavistara Text* (1926). (Interesting pictorial reproductions of Javanese conceptions.)

Mahaparinibbana Suttanta. Translated from the Pali by Rhys Davids in *SBE*, Vol. XI; also in his *Dialogs of the Buddha*, Vol. III. (Events of the last days of Buddha.)

Rockhill, W. W.: *Life of the Buddha and the Early History of His Order, Derived from Tibetan Works.*

Vinaya Texts, Mahavagga, and *Cullavagga* (SBE), Vols. XIII, XVII, and XX.

Warren, H. C.: *Buddhism in Translations* (1896), pp. 1–110.

LITERARY

Arnold, Sir Edwin: *The Light of Asia* (New York, 1894). (A poetical presentation of Buddha and his teachings by an imaginary Buddhist priest. Based on the *Lalitavistara.*)

b) Sources for the life of Buddha

1. The Pali scriptures: the canon of the Theravada
   (*a*) The earliest period at which we have evidence of the existence of a body of scriptures is 247 B.C., or two hundred and thirty-six years after the death of Buddha
   (*b*) From Chinese translations and fragments of Sanskrit works we know that there are other forms of the canon in other schools than the Theravada
   (*c*) Divisions of the Pali canon: the Tripitaka (or "Three Baskets")
      (1) Sutta Pitaka: dialogues or discourses on the doctrine
      (2) Vinaya Pitaka: disciplinary rules for the monks; biographical material here is in the commentaries attached
      (3) Abhidhamma Pitaka: scholastic elaborations of the doctrine
2. The Sanskrit tradition
   (*a*) Collections of legends preserved in the Tibetan scriptures, translated from the Sanskrit, chiefly from the Vinaya
      (1) The most important of these have been translated by Rockhill as *Life of Buddha*
   (*b*) The Mahavastu ("The Great Story")
      (1) It calls itself the Vinaya of the Lokottara branch of the Mahasanghika school; a mass of legends

(*c*) The Lalitavistara: A continuous narrative of the life of Buddha from his decision to be born down to his first sermon

(*d*) The Buddha Carita: Aims to fill up the details of the story of Buddha until the enlightenment; an epic poem by Asvaghosha

(*e*) The Abhinishkramana-sutra: Exists only in Chinese translation. Abridged in English by Beal as *The Romantic Legend of Sakya Buddha* (London, 1875).

3. Sculptured monuments

(*a*) These record mostly legendary accounts (see, for an example, Krom's work cited above)

c) A brief outline of the life of Buddha

1. He was born into one of the wealthy, aristocratic families of the Kshatriya tribe known as the Sakyas, which possessed a narrow strip of territory in North India lying between the Rapti River and the Himalaya Mountains (now in the Nepalese Tarai)

(*a*) Date of birth, *ca.* 563 B.C. (see Thomas, p. 27)

(*b*) Name of father, Suddhodana; of mother, Maya

2. Names of Buddha

(*a*) Siddhattha (Pali) or Siddhartha (Sanskrit), his personal name, means "He Who Has Accomplished His Aim"

(*b*) Gotama, or Gautama, name of his gens or family

(*c*) Buddha—"The Awakened or Wise One"; most celebrated title

(*d*) Sakya-Muni—"The Sage of the Sakyas"

(*e*) Bhagava—"Lord"

(*f*) Tathagata—"He Who Has Come Thus" (or "He Who Has Arrived")

3. Religious and moral atmosphere in which Gotama grew up

(*a*) Brahmanic influence present but not dominant in the religion

(*b*) The ideal of the religious mendicant was common

(c) Though surrounded by wealth and comfort, Buddha mused on human suffering and felt attracted to the religious life

(d) The love of wife and child did not prevail over his responsiveness to the religious environment

4. The Great Renunciation

(a) At the age of twenty-nine Buddha left his family, his wife, and infant son to adopt the wandering life and seek salvation, deliverance from rebirth (see p. 1, b, 3)

5. Austerities and enlightenment: six years of striving

(a) At Rajagaha he applied to contemporary teachers of religion

(1) But Alara Kalama could lead him no farther than to the "attainment of the state of nothingness"

(2) And Uddaka Ramaputta could lead him no farther than the "state of neither-consciousness-nor-nonconsciousness"

(b) At Uruvela he practiced the severest forms of asceticism

(1) Five monks joined him, hoping that when he had found the truth he would tell it to them

(2) But after he had fallen senseless from the severity of his self-mortifications he abandoned this method, upon which the five monks left him in disappointment

(c) Finally after practicing meditation, while seated under a Bo-tree, he attained his "great enlightenment"

(1) He understood the nature of error and of suffering, the cessation of suffering, and the path that leads to the cessation of suffering

6. The first preaching

(a) After some hesitation because of the doubt that his insight was too profound to impart, Buddha decided to teach others

(b) The first disciples were the five monks, companions of his austerities
  (1) To these he is supposed to have preached the "Sermon at Benares" and the "Sermon on the Marks of Non-soul" (see Thomas, pp. 87–89)
(c) Another early sermon was the so-called "Fire Sermon" (see Warren, pp. 351–53, for the text)

7. The first lay persons to become disciples
  (a) Yasa, son of a wealthy guildmaster; became a monk
  (b) Yasa's father, mother, and former wife became lay disciples
  (c) Then four friends of Yasa
  (d) Then fifty other friends of Yasa
8. When the number of disciples had reached sixty Buddha sent them out in different directions to preach the doctrine
  (a) The result was a great increase in numbers
    (1) Other religious leaders, even, together with their disciples joined the growing order
9. Main aspects of Buddha's forty-five years as a wandering teacher
  (a) Buddha worked out the characteristic features of his teaching
  (b) He laid down the regulations for the order of monks, and of nuns
  (c) Monasteries were built and lands given by wealthy lay adherents for the use of the monks
  (d) In Buddha's old age a schism threatened under the leadership of Devadatta, "the Buddhist Judas," but it was averted
10. The last days of Buddha (Mahaparinibbana Sutta)
  (a) Buddha seemed aware of his approaching end and spent much time in discoursing with his disciples on all that he considered important
  (b) His final illness was occasioned by eating some pork served him by Cunda, a smith who was his host at Pava

(c) He died at Kusinara, at the age of eighty (483 B.C.)

(1) His last words were: "Now then, monks, I address you; subject to decay are all compound things. Strive with earnestness."

(2) The funeral rites were performed by the Mallas of Kusinara

(3) The ashes were divided into eight parts as relics for eight different groups of claimants

NOTE.—For the sake of brevity the foregoing outline takes no account of the legendary material which has gathered about almost every aspect of the life. But this material as revealing the attitudes of the ancient Buddhist world is significant.

III. The Teaching of Buddha

a) References

Cave, Sydney Cave: *Living Religions of the East*, pp. 114–28. (A good, clear, brief account.)

Coomaraswamy, Ananda: *Buddha and the Gospel of Buddhism*, pp. 90–151. (Popular in style but suggestive.)

Dasgupta, Surendranath: *History of Indian Philosophy*, I, 82–109. (A valuable exposition by an Indian author; technical in style but helpful for the discrimination of terms.)

Davids, T. W. Rhys: *Buddhism: Its History and Literature*, pp. 118–86.

Eliot, Sir Charles: *Hinduism and Buddhism*, Vol. I, Book III, chap. x on "The Teaching of Buddha." (Wise appreciation.)

ERE: Articles on "Karma," "Nirvana," "Transmigration," etc.

Farquhar, J. N.: *An Outline of the Religious Literature of India*, pp. 63–65. (Excellent, succinct statement.)

Keith, A. Berriedale: *Buddhist Philosophy*, Part I, pp. 13–146 on "Buddhism in the Pali Canon." (A thoroughgoing treatment by a noted Sanskrit scholar; presupposes considerable knowledge of the literature.)

Moore, G. F.: *History of Religions*, I, 291–98.

Oldenberg, H.: *Buddha: Sein Leben, seine Lehre, seine Gemeinde*, pp. 208–337. (An old presentation, still valuable.)

Oltramare, Paul: *La théosophie bouddhique* (1923). (The latest comprehensive statement by a French scholar.)

Radhakrishnan, S.: *Indian Philosophy*, I, 362–476. (Interesting treatment by an Indian author who uses freely Western parallels and interpretations.)

Saunders: *Epochs in Buddhist History* (cf. p. 8, bottom of page.)

Thomas, E. J.: *Life of Buddha*, pp. 173–210.

Vallée-Poussin, L. de la: *Way to Nirvana*. (Presents the teaching as a discipline of salvation.)

Warren, H. C.: *Buddhism in Translations* (abbreviated below as *WBT*), pp. 111–391.

b) Buddha's teaching in outline
- 1. The problem was a therapeutic one
  - (*a*) To find the cause and the cure of misery
- 2. Buddha's solution: the knowledge and practice of
  - (*a*) The Four Noble Truths
    - (1) Existence is suffering
    - (2) The origin of suffering is desire (which leads to rebirth)
    - (3) The cessation of suffering is the cessation of desire
    - (4) The way to the cessation of desire is the eightfold path, which is the middle path between indulgence and useless austerities (see [*b*])
  - (*b*) The Noble Eightfold Path (after Digha Nikaya, *WBT*, pp. 368–75)
    - (1) Right belief—knowledge of misery, its cause, its cessation, and the path
    - (2) Right resolve—to renounce sensual pleasure, to have malice toward none, to harm no living creatures

(3) Right speech—to abstain from falsehood, backbiting, and harsh language
(4) Right behavior—to abstain from destroying life, from taking what is not given one, from immorality
(5) Right occupation—to quit a wrong occupation and follow a right one
(6) Right effort—mental effort to keep the mind free of evil mental qualities and to retain good ones (see *WBT*, p. 373)
(7) Right contemplation (or mindfulness)—to be alert with regard to the body sensations, ideas, etc. (see *ibid.*, p. 374)
(8) Right concentration (or rapture)
  (*a*) The first trance
    (1) Produced by isolation
    (2) Characterized by joy and happiness
  (*b*) The second trance
    (1) An interior tranquillization and intentness of the thoughts
    (2) Produced by concentration
  (*c*) The third trance
    (1) Indifferent, contemplative, with an experience of bodily happiness
  (*d*) The fourth trance
    (1) Gained through the abandonment of happiness, the abandonment of misery, the disappearance of all antecedent gladness or grief
    (2) A state of neither happiness nor misery, which is "contemplation refined by indifference"

3. Three other important conceptions
  (*a*) The doctrine of *anatta* (non-soul or non-ego) (for texts see *WBT*, chap. ii, pp. 111–208)

(1) A seeming contradiction in Buddha's teaching about personality
  (*a*) There is no self (*attan* in Pali, *atman* in Sanskrit) in the sense of a permanent, unitary entity; what we ordinarily call a self is a compound of material and mental qualities (called *khandas* in Pali, *skandhas* in Sanskrit)
  (*b*) There is, however, reward of actions in a future existence
  (*c*) How, then, can the individual feel responsible for his deeds?

(2) Attempts to explain the contradiction
  (*a*) Warren says that "rebirth is not transmigration" (pp. 234–38)
  (*b*) Barth says that the dead Buddhist does not revive but another revives in his stead (see Poussin, p. 49)
  (*c*) Poussin interprets the Buddhist solution to be that the revived person is continuous with the old one in the sense that the individual is an unbroken series of changing states
    (1) Similes: milk changing to curds, persons growing old, fire spreading, the candle flame continuously burning, etc.
  (*d*) Farquhar, however, thinks that Poussin's explanation implies the annihilation of the emancipated priest at death (p. 65)
    (1) But this is expressly denied (*WBT*, pp. 138–46)
    (2) He suggests that Buddha, while maintaining both the doctrine of no-soul, on the one hand, and transmigration and deliverance, on the other, did not try to reconcile the notions philosophically

(*b*) The doctrine of *karma* (*ibid.*, chap. iii, pp. 209–79)
  (1) Not original with Buddhism

(a) It appears in the Upanishads, though apparently as an esoteric doctrine (Eliot, I, 94)
(b) It was also known to the Jains (*ibid.*, p. 107, and Dasgupta, p. 73)
(c) The Jatilas, ascetics, who joined Buddha's order already believed in *karma*

(2) The doctrine arises out of a sentiment of justice
(a) It explains inequality in the world (*WBT*, pp. 214–15)

(3) With Buddha it was a wholly moral conception
(a) Not linked with a metaphysical-soul theory as in the Upanishads
(b) Nor with materialistic conception as in Jainism.
(c) It was the "law of the deed," an impersonal, universal principle of moral cause and effect

(4) Its practical significance
(a) The responsibility for the consequences of moral conduct is upon the individual, not upon something outside himself
(b) Taken in conjunction with the dynamic conception of personality, it maintains the possibility of the remaking of character, and the power of the individual to shape his own future

(c) Nirvana

(1) In its primary meaning the word is derived from a verb which signifies "to go out," as a lamp goes out when the oil is exhausted
(a) The reference is to the extinction of the desire and attachment which leads to rebirth (see *ibid.*, p. 380)
(b) As a state it is one of calm joy and inner peace

(2) Does the saint who has attained Nirvana exist in some condition other than *samsara*, the realm of rebirth; or is he completely annihilated at death?

(3) Buddha himself refused to answer the question. Both answers have been given by his followers (see Saunders, *Epochs in Buddhist History*, pp. 14–18, and Keith, pp. 61–68)

IV. The Early Order

a) References

Cave, S.: *Living Religions of the East*, pp. 129–31.

Copleston, Reginald S.: *Buddhism, Primitive and Present in Magadha and Ceylon*, pp. 119–49.

Davids, T. W. Rhys: *Dialogs of the Buddha*, Parts I and II. (Source material. Instances of formation of regulations, etc.)

Dutt, Sukumar: *Early Buddhist Monachism* (1924). Pp. 197. (The most detailed recent study, showing the order as a developing social process.)

Eliot, Sir Charles: *Hinduism and Buddhism*, I, 237–53. (A good picture of the early monastic life.)

Geden, A. S.: Article in *ERE*, VIII, 797–802, on "Buddhist Monasticism." (Good comprehensive account.)

Hackmann, H.: *Buddhism as a Religion*, pp. 27–31.

Hardy, R. Spence: *Eastern Monachism* (1850). (A standard older reference.)

Kern, J. H. C.: *Manual of Indian Buddhism* (1896), pp. 73–101. (Also by an older authority.)

Monier-Williams, Monier: *Buddhism*, pp. 71–92.

Moore, G. F.: *History of Religions*, I, 298–301. (Convenient brief account.)

Warren, H. C.: *Buddhism in Translations* [*WBT*], pp. 393–486. (Valuable selections from the sources concerning the order.)

b) Essential points concerning the order

1. The monastic order was not original with Buddha
   (*a*) It was common for religious teachers with many disciples to organize them into regulated communities
2. The distinctive features of Buddha's order
   (*a*) It removed all restrictions of class

- (*b*) It placed upon all alike the same requirements
- (*c*) It was probably less prone to extravagances (of the ascetic sort) and better organized

3. The monks had no fixed abode
   - (*a*) They followed the wandering life of the mendicant
   - (*b*) Only during the rainy seasons did they remain in a definite place or in a permanent building
4. Restrictions of entrance into the order
   - (*a*) Those suffering from mental or bodily defect, the vicious, gamblers, debtors, minors without the consent of parents, were not admitted
5. There were regulations covering
   - (*a*) The ceremony of admission to the order (see *WBT*, pp. 393–401)
   - (*b*) The equipment of the monk; alms bowl, vestments, staff razor, toothpick, water-strainer (to prevent unwitting taking of insect life), etc.
   - (*c*) The reception of converts from other sects
   - (*d*) Activities of the monks
     - (1) Daily routine, such as
       - (*a*) Recitation and prayers
       - (*b*) Going the rounds for alms
       - (*c*) Partaking of the simple noonday meal, with rest and meditation following
       - (*d*) Evening service and recitations in the temple or hall of the monastery
     - (2) Other activities
       - (*a*) Regular instruction to the junior monks (*sramaneras*)
       - (*b*) Preaching during the rainy season to the laymen
       - (*c*) Bimonthly Uposatha days (days of abstinence and fasting)
         - (1) At this time the Pratimoksha, or confession of sin, was formally recited
         - (2) "The only distinct instance of united de-

vout activity of the whole community" (Hackmann, p. 31)

6. The vows were not irrevocable
   (*a*) The monk was free at any time without blame to discard his robes and return to the world
7. Provision for the lay Buddhists
   (*a*) Those admitted to the monastery as laborers and servants
      (1) A less strict discipline than that of the monks
   (*b*) The outside laity who visited the monasteries and made offerings at shrines
      (1) They were to abstain from taking life, drinking intoxicants, lying, stealing, and unchastity
      (2) In addition they might win special merit by using no garlands or perfumes, sleeping on a mat spread on the ground, and not eating after midday
      (3) In stories illustrating the right life of the layman
         (*a*) There is emphasis on the social virtues, such as pleasant speech, kindness, temperance, consideration for others, and affection
         (*b*) There is commendation for almsgiving, religious conversation, hearing of the law
         (*c*) Mutual duties are enjoined in relations of
            (1) Parents and children
            (2) Pupils and teachers
            (3) Husband and wife
            (4) Friend and friend
            (5) Masters and servants
            (6) Laity and clergy
8. The rules of poverty did not apply to monasteries in their corporate capacity
   (*a*) The monasteries were wealthy and influential through
      (1) Gifts of land
      (2) Revenues from estates or villages granted in perpetuity by wealthy patrons

(3) Gifts of money, buildings, etc.

9. The order of nuns
   (*a*) Never very popular or numerous
   (*b*) The rules for the nuns involved obedience to the order of monks in all respects
      (1) A nun even of a hundred years' standing was to rise and respectfully salute even the youngest monk
      (2) A nun could not keep Vassa in a district in which no monk was resident, etc.

V. Early Conferences or Councils

a) References

Eliot, Sir Charles: *Hinduism and Buddhism*, I, 254–63. (On the whole, the most readable account.)

Franke, R. O.: "The Buddhist Councils at Rajagaha and Vesali," *Journal of the Pali Text Society*, 1908. (A very close examination of the sources on the two first councils, with the conclusion that they never happened, at least as Buddhists understood them.)

McGovern, W. M.: *Introduction to Mahayana Buddhism*, pp. 185–87.

Moore, George F.: *History of Religions*, I, 301–4.

Oltramare, Paul: *L'histoire des idées théosophiques dans l'Inde* (1923), Vol. II: *La théosophie bouddhique*, pp. 64–77. (See below.)

Thomas, E. J.: *Life of Buddha*, pp. 165–72. (Recent account.)

Vallée-Poussin, L. de la: "Les conciles bouddhiques," *Museon* (1905). Translated in *Indian Antiquary* (1908). (A thorough study by a master.)

Vallée-Poussin, L. de la: Article on "Councils (Buddhist)" in *ERE*, Vol. IV. (A presentation of practically the present state of our knowledge on the subject.)

Winternitz, M.: Article on "Most Ancient Buddhist Records," in Nariman's *Literary History of Sanskrit Buddhism*, pp. 207–11.

ORIGINAL SOURCES

Cullavagga, XI, XII, SBE, Vol. XX.
The *Dipavamsa.*
The *Mahavamsa.* (See below, p. 40.)
Przyluski, Jean: *Le concile de Rājagṛha: Introduction à l'histoire des canons et des sectes bouddhiques* (1926). (Contains translations of pertinent Chinese texts.)

b) Interest attaching to the councils
  1. They witness to differences of opinion in matters of both faith and practice and the attempt to come to some agreement

c) But there is considerable uncertainty in our knowledge about them
  1. The oldest authority dates from a century or two after the first council (see Thomas, p. 165)
  2. There are discrepancies and improbabilities in the accounts
    (*a*) This does not, however, preclude their containing a kernel of historic truth

d) The traditional councils
  1. The first: at Rajagaha
    (*a*) Said to have been held immediately after Buddha's death when five hundred monks spent the rainy season together and chanted the suttas and the vinaya, thus fixing their authority
  2. The Council of Vesali (one hundred or one hundred and ten years after Buddha's death)
    (*a*) A council to examine (and which condemned) ten extra-legal practices of the monks at Vesali
    (*b*) The Dipavamsa says that the condemned monks held a rival council of 10,000 members and founded a separate sect
  3. The Council at Pataliputra
    (*a*) Held under King Asoka (Sinhalese sources say two hundred and thirty-six years after Buddha)
    (*b*) Apparently a discussion of five controverted ques-

tions; these are in the Sinhalese Katthavatthu, which is a catalogue of heresies

(c) There is no record of this council in the accounts of northern Buddhism

4. The Council at Jalandhara, second century A.D. (time of Kanishka)

(a) Northern Buddhism accepts the tradition that the addition of Sanskrit commentaries to the canon was sanctioned at this time

(b) But the Pali sources are silent about this council

e) Oltramare takes the position that the tradition of councils which settled certain doctrinal questions was an invention springing out of the needs of limited groups, seeking to give authority to their own positions (pp. 64–77)

VI. Asoka, Imperial Patron of World-Buddhism

a) References

Davids, T. W. Rhys: *Buddhist India*, Index, "Asoka."

Eliot, Sir Charles: *Hinduism and Buddhism*, I, 263–74.

Kennedy: "Buddhist Gnosticism," *Journal of the Royal Asiatic Society*, 1902, pp. 377–415.

Saunders, Kenneth J.: *Epochs in Buddhist History*, pp. 29–34.

Smith, Vincent A.: *Asoka, the Buddhist Emperor of India.* (The fullest treatment in English. Gives the history of Asoka, descriptions of the monuments, translations of the rock and pillar edicts, and the Ceylonese and Indian legends.)

Smith, Vincent A.: Article on "Asoka" in *ERE*, Vol. II. (A convenient reference.)

Smith, Vincent A.: *Early History of India, Including Alexander's Campaigns*, chap. vi, pp. 143–83. (A briefer treatment.)

Thomas, F. W.: "Asoka, the Imperial Patron of Buddhism," *Cambridge History of India*, pp. 495–513.

b) Main facts concerning Asoka in connection with Buddhism

1. Asoka (273–231 B.C.), one of the greatest of Indian emperors, was a patron and adherent of Buddhism
2. His significance in Buddhist history
   (a) He transformed an obscure local sect in the basin of the Ganges into a dominant world-religion
3. His life
   (a) He was the grandson of Chandragupta Maurya, the first emperor of India, and son of Bindusara
   (b) Asoka inherited a vast empire (see Smith, *Early History*, p. 150), which he rounded off by the conquest of the kingdom of Kalinga, which is on the coast of Bengal between the Mahanadi and Godavari rivers
   (c) Conscience-stricken at the horrors of this war of conquest, and coming under the influence of Buddhist teachers about the same time, he determined to become a man of peace and devote his energies to spreading the Dhamma (really his conception of the Buddhist ethical teaching)
   (d) His activities in behalf of Buddhism
      (1) Enforced respect for the sanctity of animal life
         (a) Abolished the royal hunt in 259 B.C.
         (b) Stopped the butchery of animals for the royal table
         (c) In 243 B.C. issued detailed regulations concerning the slaughter or mutilation of animals
      (2) Preached before his subjects in order to give them a good example
      (3) In 249 B.C. made a solemn pilgrimage to the most sacred spots in the Buddhist Holy Land
      (4) Caused his ethical preaching (Dhamma) to be carved on rocks, bowlders, cave walls, and pillars
         (a) Thirty-five distinct documents preserved to us
            (1) Fourteen rock edicts (translated in Smith's "Asoka"), dating from the thirteenth and fourteenth years of his reign
            (2) Seven pillar inscriptions (engraved on

sandstone monoliths), from the twenty-seventh and twenty-eighth years of his reign
- (3) Other lesser inscriptions
- (b) The primary duties of the Asokan code
  - (1) Respect for the right of animals to life
  - (2) Reverence for parents, elders, and preceptors
  - (3) Truthfulness
- (5) Promoted the missionary spread of Buddhism (see below)
- (6) In his life displayed great energy, combining the piety of a saint with the practical qualities of an able king
- (7) In 240 B.C. Asoka was ordained as a monk, though without abdicating the throne
- (e) Asoka died in either 232 or 231 B.C.

4. Asoka's missionary work
   - (a) In India
     - (1) Required officials in government to give moral instruction to those below them
     - (2) Appointed censors as a special class
       - (a) To promote piety among people of all sects
       - (b) To superintend the female establishments of members of the royal family
       - (c) To prevent wrongful imprisonment or corporal punishment
       - (d) To function among the bordering tribes and nations subject to Asoka's suzerainty
   - (b) Outside India
     - (1) Ceylon
       - (a) It was evangelized with permanent success by a group of missionaries under Asoka's younger brother, Mahinda
     - (2) Western countries: Buddhist missionaries were sent to

(*a*) Syria and Western Asia (then under Antiochos Theos)
(*b*) Egypt (then under Ptolemy Philadelphos)
(*c*) Cyrene (under Magas)
(*d*) Epirus (under Alexander)
(*e*) Macedonia (under Antigonos Gonatas)

(*c*) Effects of missionary effort
(1) The movement did not succeed in establishing branch churches except in Ceylon
(2) But it affected the Gnostic and Manichean sects of Christianity (see Kennedy, "Buddhist Gnosticism," *Journal of the Royal Asiatic Society*, for 1902, pp. 377–415)
(3) *In reflex action on India it helped to develop the Mahayana form of Buddhism*
(4) For many centuries made Buddhist institutions a prominent feature of Indian life
(5) Led ultimately to the extension of Buddhism to Tibet, China, and Japan

5. Asoka's greatness: "As a king he disputes with Akbar the right to the highest place of honor among the sovereigns of India, and, in the history of Buddhism, his importance is second only to that of the founder of the system."—Smith, *ERE*, II, 127.

VII. Growth and Transformation of Buddhism in India: Rise of the Mahayana

a) References

Davids, T. W. Rhys: *Buddhism: Its History and Literature*, pp. 187–212.

Eliot, Sir Charles: *Hinduism and Buddhism*, II, 3–6 and 63–82.

ERE: Article on "Mahayana" by L. de la Vallée-Poussin. (Good on the doctrinal changes and characteristics.)

Farquhar, J. N.: *Outline of the Religious Literature of India*, pp. 111–12.

Foucher, A.: *The Beginnings of Buddhist Art.* (See especially Lecture IV on "The Greek Origin of the Image of Buddha.")

Hackmann, H.: *Buddhism as a Religion*, pp. 48–56. (Clear and brief.)

Johnston, R. F.: *Buddhist China*, pp. 23–35. (A good statement by a special student of the Chinese Mahayana.)

McGovern, William M.: *Introduction to Mahayana Buddhism*, pp. 16–20.

Moore, G. F.: *History of Religions*, I, 304–6.

Radhakrishnan, S.: *Indian Philosophy*, I, 589–605. (Describes the difference between Hinayana and Mahayana branches of Buddhism.)

Reischauer, A. K.: *Studies in Japanese Buddhism*, pp. 57–70. (Good brief treatment.)

Saunders, K. J.: *Epochs in Buddhist History*, pp. 47–69.

Smith, V. A.: *Early History of India*, pp. 239–51. (Especially for the life of Kanishka and the council held during his reign.)

b) Outline of main points

1. A great change came over Buddhism in North India after Asoka's time, especially during the first and second centuries A.D.
   (*a*) The ideal of the Arhat was replaced by that of the Bodhisattva
      (1) The Arhat was one who wins Nirvana by a strenuous discipline at once and who will not again be born
      (2) The Bodhisattva is one who reaches release by means of a devotion to others in a long career reaching through endless lives; he foregoes Nirvana for the sake of others.
   (*b*) Buddhas and Bodhisattvas came to be regarded as supernatural beings, in time worshiped as deities
   (*c*) Gotama was regarded as simply one earthly manifes-

tation of a cosmic Buddha essence that has incarnated itself countless times in the past and will do so yet countless times in the future; and that reveals itself also in heavenly Buddhas who rule paradises in other worlds

(*d*) Emphasis came to be placed on salvation by faith in some Bodhisattva

(1) Invocation of the name of Amitabha secures rebirth in his paradise, etc.

2. Causes of the change

(*a*) Internal, within India

(1) Continued growth of Indian thought; the interest in metaphysics kept developing beyond the limits set down by Buddha

(2) The need of the people for a more emotional morality and more personal, sympathetic deities

(3) The influence of other Indian religious thought and practice. According to Saunders these are

(*a*) The Sankhya philosophy

(*b*) Polytheistic Hinduism (as expressed in the Bhagavadgita)

(*c*) The monism of Vedanta

(*d*) Yoga

(*b*) External, coming from outside India

(1) Northwest India was invaded by many different foreign peoples at different times

(*a*) Persians, Greeks (whose influence stimulated the growth of mythology and imagery; see Foucher above), Parthians, Sakas, and Kushans

(*b*) The foreign converts naturally brought in other ideas which mixed with those of Buddhism. Smith goes so far as to say (p. 248).:

(1) "Mahayana was largely of foreign origin, and its development was the result of the

complex interaction of Indian, Zoroastrian, Gnostic and Hellenic elements."

3. Kanishka's council, second century A.D. (see p. 18 above). (Kanishka was the most famous of the Indo-Scythian kings and held sway over the Kushan Empire, possibly from 78 to 120 A.D. The dates are much debated.)
   (*a*) Five hundred monks met at Jalandhara in Kashmir
   (*b*) They examined all the theological literature and elaborated commentaries on the three pitakas
   (*c*) The works included the Mahavibhasha, which still exists in Chinese
   (*d*) The commentaries thus prepared were copied on sheets of copper, which were deposited in a *stupa* built for the purpose by Kanishka
   (*e*) This council seems to have been Hinayanist, but its account by Hsuan Chwang bears witness to the presence of the new Mahayanist tendencies (see Beal, *Buddhist Records*, I, 153, also Johnston, p. 33)
4. Literary masterpieces of the period (after Saunders)
   (*a*) *Milinda Panha:* which, though generally Hinayanist, contains the germ of the Mahayana doctrines of salvation by faith and Bodhisattvas; translated in "Sacred Books of the East"
   (*b*) *Lalita-vistara* (see Krom, cited on p. 3 above)
   (*c*) *Sutralamkara:* a collection of Mahayanist legends
   (*d*) *Sukhavati Vyuha Sutras:* Descriptions of the western paradise of Amitabha (SBE, Vol. XLIX)
   (*e*) *Saddharma Pundarika* ("Lotus of the True Law"): the greatest exposition of the whole Mahayana system (*ibid.*, Vol. XXI)
5. This new, transformed Buddhism called itself the "Mahayana"
   (*a*) Mahayana means "The Great Vehicle," that is, the great conveyance to salvation
   (*b*) Hinayana means "The Little Vehicle," or little conveyance to salvation

(1) It was a term used by the Mahayanists to designate the older, more conservative type of Buddhism that still persisted

6. Eliot's characterizations of Mahayana and Hinayana

(*a*) Mahayana was less monastic; more emotional; warmer in charity; more personal in devotion; more ornate in art, literature, and ritual; more disposed to evolution and development

(*b*) Hinayana was conservative and rigid; secluded in its cloisters; and open to the plausible if unjust accusation of selfishness (II, 4)

VIII. Philosophical Development of the Mahayana

a) References

Anesaki, M.: Article on "Asanga" in *ERE*, Vol. II. (Contains a clear brief statement of the idealist [Vijnanavada] school.)

Coomaraswamy, Ananda: *Buddha and the Gospel of Buddhism*, pp. 226–52. (More descriptive than analytical.)

Dasgupta, Surendranath: *History of Indian Philosophy*, I, 125–51. (A thoroughgoing exposition of the Mahayanist systems; well worth studying.)

Eliot, Sir Charles: *Hinduism and Buddhism*, II, 36–46. (A discussion rather than an exposition.)

Farquhar, J. N.: *Outline of the Religious Literature of India*, pp. 112–18, 157–62.

Keith, A. B.: *Buddhist Philosophy in India and Ceylon*, pp. 216–302. (Painstaking, systematic statement with exhaustive utilization of available sources.)

Kern, H.: *Manual of Indian Buddhism*, pp. 126 ff.

McGovern, William M.: *Introduction to Mahayana Buddhism*, pp. 20–24.

Moore, George F.: *History of Religions*, I, 306–10.

Nariman, G. K.: *Literary History of Sanskrit Buddhism*, chap. viii, pp. 89–109.

Pratt, James Bissett: *The Pilgrimage of Buddhism* (1928), pp. 234–70. (Discussed with a philosopher's insight.)

Radhakrishnan, S.: *Indian Philosophy*, I, 624–69. (Readable; vivid. Makes free comparisons with Western systems of thought.)

Saunders, K. J.: *Epochs in Buddhist History*, pp. 70–104. (Interesting discussion of the philosophical along with several other phases of the developed Mahayana.)

Suzuki, D. T.: *Outlines of Mahayana Buddhism*, pp. 21 ff., 62 ff.

Vallée-Poussin, L. de la: Article on "Madhyamaka" in *ERE*, VIII, 235–37.

Vallée-Poussin, L. de la: *Bouddhisme*, pp. 186–204. (Shows the logical evolution of the nihilist and idealist systems out of their Hinayanist antecedents.)

Pratt, James Bissett: *The Pilgrimage of Buddhism* (1928), pp. 234–70. (Discussed with a philosopher's insight.)

Yamakami, Sōgen: *Systems of Buddhist Thought*, pp. 186–251. (An elaborate treatment by a Japanese scholar. Its many quotations are suggestive.)

SOURCES AVAILABLE IN WESTERN TRANSLATIONS

Akutobhaya, by Nagarjuna. German translation from the Tibetan by Walleser, *Die mittlere Lehre des Nagarjuna.*

Asvaghosha: *Awakening of Faith.* English translation by Suzuki.

Diamond Sutra (*Vajracchedika*). Eng. translation in SBE, Vol. XLIX.

Life of Vasubandhu, by Paramartha. Eng. translation by Takakusu in *T'oung Pao*, V (1904), 269–96.

Madhyamakavatara. French translation from the Tibetan by Poussin, *Le museon*, Vols. VIII and IX.

Mahayana-Sutralamkara, by Asanga. French translation by S. Levi.

Prajna-Paramita-Hridaya, in *SBE*, Vol. XLIX.

Saddharma Pundarika Sutra, in *ibid.*, Vol. XXI.

Santideva: Siksha-Samuccaya. English translation by Bendall and Rouse. (A compendium of Buddhist doctrine compiled chiefly from earlier Mahayana *sutras.*)

Sutralamkara, by Asvaghosha. French translation by Huber. Paris, 1908.

Vijnaptimatratasiddhi, by Vasubandhu. French translation from the Chinese by Poussin (Paris, 1928).

Vimsakakarikaprakarana. French translation from the Tibetan by Poussin in *op. cit.* (1912).

b) Outline of the development of Mahayana philosophy

1. The period from 200–550 A.D. was a time when all the great religious movements in India (Hindu, Jain, and Buddhist) sought to give philosophical expression to their ideas
2. This was made possible in part by the peace and prosperity of North India under the Gupta dynasty, which lasted from 320 until 647 A.D. (see Farquhar, p. 122)
3. Two main schools came to be differentiated in the Mahayana
   - (*a*) Madhyamaka: founded by Nagarjuna (flourished second century A.D.)
     - (1) Elements in early Buddhism which were the germs from which Madhyamaka grew
       - (*a*) Buddha's doctrine of the middle path
       - (*b*) The doctrine that there is no permanent individual
       - (*c*) The doctrine that every individual is made up of elements (*dharmas*) which are momentary and perishing though real while they last
     - (2) The Madhyamaka teaching
       - (*a*) The *dharmas* as well as the individual are unreal ("Everything is void")
       - (*b*) Existence is a continuous procession of illusory, unreal *dharmas*
       - (*c*) Our acceptance of them as real is due to ignorance

(*d*) The only knowledge that can arrest the renewal of *dharmas* is knowledge of their radical and fundamental unreality

(*e*) Madhyamaka interpretations (see Poussin in *ERE* cited above)

(1) Nirvana is the end of the production of these phenomena

(2) Impurity is attachment to phenomena conceived as pleasant

(3) Purity is complete detachment from phenomena

(4) Ignorance is a clinging to the substantiality of phenomena which induces attachment

(5) Wisdom is the real truth, knowledge of the vacuity of things

(*f*) Extreme positions

(1) The object described, the description, and the person describing are all similarly nonexistent

(2) "Absolute truth is silence"

(*b*) Yogacarya (or Vijnanavada) school

(1) Founded by Asanga and Vasubandhu in the fourth century A.D.

(2) Agreements with the Madhyamaka teaching (Dasgupta, p. 145)

(*a*) All the *dharmas* are but the constructions of ignorant minds

(*b*) There is no movement in the external world, for it does not exist

(*c*) We construct it ourselves and then are deluded that it exists by itself

(*d*) All our phenomenal knowledge is without any essence or truth and is but a creation of *maya*, a mirage or a dream

(3) Distinctive conceptions

(*a*) All phenomena, both material and non-material, originate in mind

(*b*) Mind according to its action reveals eight functions or consciousnesses

(1) Visual consciousness

(2) Oral consciousness

(3) Nasal consciousness

(4) Consciousness of objects of taste

(5) Consciousness of objects of touch

(6) The consciousness which discriminates between the various phenomena of the universe

(7) The consciousness which distinguishes between subject and object (we would say "self-consciousness")

(8) The receptacle consciousness (Alaya Vijnana)

(*c*) The seeds or possibilities of all phenomena are contained in the eighth or receptacle consciousness

(1) When they grow and unfold there springs up the distinction of subject and object and the illusory multiplicity of an objective world

(2) In consequence of this we are disturbed and rove about in search of peace, suffering the pain of attachment to this and that transient thing

(3) If we once fully understand that nothing else exists but mind, then the objective world ceases to exist for us, and the eight confused consciousnesses are turned into eight kinds of enlightened wisdom by means of which we can unite with the ultimate which transcends speech and thought

- (4) The Alaya Vijnana is the ocean; the whole phenomenal world is but the waves resulting from its operations

(c) In the awakening of faith (ascribed to Asvaghosha) there is a special form of the Vijnanavada

- (1) This is of special interest, for it has been particularly influential in China and Japan
- (2) Three main conceptions (according to Suzuki)
  - (a) Suchness (*bhutatathata*)
    - (1) It is a universal soul which is the "oneness of the totality of things," the absolute spiritual reality (*Awakening of Faith* [Suzuki's trans.], p. 55)
    - (2) In its own essence this spiritual absolute is pure and at rest
    - (3) But aroused by ignorance its activity produces the illusory multiplicity of the phenomenal world; it is then called "defiled mind"
    - (4) The recognition that suchness is the only true reality is Nirvana
  - (b) The theory of triple personality
    - (1) Dharmakaya, or "Body of the Law"; the absolute in itself
    - (2) Nirmanakaya, or "Body of Transformation"; the absolute as embodied in earthly Buddhas
    - (3) Sambhogakaya, or "Body of Bliss"; the absolute as embodied in heavenly Buddhas
- (3) Salvation by faith (i.e., in Amitabha Buddha, in whose paradise the believer will then be born) (see *ibid.*, p. 146)

4. Biographical references on the great names connected with the Mahayana philosophy

(*a*) Asvaghosha
Anesaki, M.: Article on "Asvaghosha" in *ERE*, Vol. II. Levi, Sylvain: "Asvaghosha le Sutralankara et ses sources," *Journal asiatique*, 1908, p. 10; XII, 77 ff.

(*b*) Nagarjuna
Anesaki, M.: Article on "Docetism" in *ERE*, IV, 838. Walleser, M.: "The Life of Nagarjuna from Tibetan and Chinese Sources," *Hirth Anniversary Volume*, pp. 421–55.

(*c*) Asanga
Anesaki, M.: Article on "Asanga" in *ERE*, Vol. II; Paramartha's *Life of Vasubandhu*. Translated in *T'oung Pao*, 1904, pp. 269 ff., by J. Takakusu. Some passages refer to Asanga, who was Vasubandhu's brother.

(*d*) Vasubandhu
Takakusu, J.: Paramartha's *Life of Vasubandhu* (just cited). Takakusu, J.: "A Study of Paramartha's *Life of Vasubandhu* and the Date of Vasubandhu," *Journal of the Royal Asiatic Society*, January, 1905.
Wogihara, U.: Article on "Vasubandhu" in *ERE*, Vol. XII.
Peri, N.: "Apropos de la date de Vasubandhu," *Bulletin de l'Ecole Française d' Extrême-Orient*, XI, 911.

NOTE.—For all four of the foregoing names Hsüan Chwang's account of his travels contains scattered references that are worth noting, for his work is one of the most important sources in Buddhist history. See *Buddhist Records* (Beal's trans.), Index.

IX. LATER INDIAN BUDDHISM AS DESCRIBED BY THE CHINESE PILGRIMS, 405–695 A.D.

a) References
S. Beal. *Buddhist Records of the Western World*. Translated from the Chinese. 2 vols. (Contains accounts of their travels and observations by Fa-Hsien, Sung Yün,

and Hsüan Chwang, who made special journeys to India to secure Buddhist books.)

Eliot, Sir Charles: *Hinduism and Buddhism*, II, 90–106. (A good summary description.)

Hackmann, H.: *Buddhism as a Religion*, pp. 57–63. (Very brief.)

Hwui-Li: *The Life of Hiuen-Tsiang.* Translated by S. Beal. (A biography by a disciple which in many places clarifies and supplements the record of the master.)

I-Tsing: *A Record of the Buddhist Religion as Practised in India and the Malay Archipelago (A.D. 671–95).* (Contains a clear description of the sects of the day and an especially full account of the regulations and practices of the monks.)

Saunders, K. J.: *Epochs in Buddhist History*, pp. 73–76. (Describes the University of Nalanda as seen by the pilgrims.)

Smith, V. A.: *Early History of India*, pp. 279–84, 315–30. (Notes especially the political suggestions in the Chinese narratives.)

The Travels of Fa-Hsien (399–414), *or Record of the Buddhistic Kingdoms.* Retrans. by H. A. Giles (1923). (Most readable. Map of journey at back.)

Watters, Thomas: *On Yüan Chwang's Travels in India.* 2 vols. (An extensive collection of very valuable notes on the life and travels of Hsüan Chwang. A most useful reference on specific questions.)

For a present-day description of the Central-Asian territory through which the pilgrims passed on their way to India read the fascinating *Ruins of Desert Cathay*, by M. Aurel Stein, being two large volumes with numerous illustrations, color plates, panoramas, and maps. Stein refers many times to Hsüan Chwang whom he calls his "patron saint."

b) Outline: Indian Buddhism seen by Chinese pilgrims

1. Fa-Hsien (traveled from 399 to 414 A.D.)

(a) Found Buddhism strong and prosperous
  (1) Monasteries were numerous, both Hinayanist and Mahayanist
    (a) Especially in places connected with the life and legends of Gotama, or at least near them in cases where old sites had been abandoned
  (2) Architecture and decorations of monasteries and *stupas* were often magnificent
  (3) Miracles, magic, and legends were an intimate part of the beliefs of both monks and laity.
  (4) Relics of Buddha were reverenced. Tooth, skull-bone, begging bowl, etc. (see Giles trans., pp. 14–17)
  (5) Subordinate elements of Indian mythology such as *deva* and *naga* worship were mingled with Buddhism (see Hackmann, p. 58; Giles trans., p. 27)
  (6) Occupations of the monks
    (a) Chanting, meditation, ascetic performances
    (b) Performance of religious ceremonies and processions
  (7) Part played by the laity
    (a) They provided for the maintenance of the priests and treated them with reverence
    (b) In return they expected blessings on their houses, families, and future

2. Sung-yün and Hui-Sheng: visited Udyana and Gandhara during the time of the Hun domination (518–21 A.D.)
  (a) This brief record, apart from the pious legends recounted, does not add greatly to the picture of Indian Buddhism of the period, but it testifies to the rudeness of the Barbarian rulers and presages the later uncertain political conditions that surrounded Buddhism in its decline (see Beal, *Records*, I, lxxxiv-cviii, and Eliot, II, 96)

3. Hsüan Chwang (his travels lasted from 629 to 645 A.D.)
  (a) The general picture is one of decline and decay

(1) Monasteries, though numerous, were often deserted or tenanted by but few priests (see Beal, I, 91, 98, 120, 137, etc., for examples)

(2) In Gandhara, most of the people belonged to heretical schools (*ibid.*, p. 98)

(3) In Udyana, there were ten *deva* temples while the Buddhist monasteries were desolate (*ibid.*, pp. 120–21)

(4) In Nepal, Buddhist and *deva* temples were closely joined and Buddhists and heretics intermingled (*ibid.*, II, 81)

(5) In Magadha, while Buddhism was still profoundly respected, unbelievers were numerous (*ibid.*, p. 82)

(6) Nalanda University, however, was filled with student priests to the number of several thousand (*ibid.*, p. 170)

(7) Kosala presented a mixture of Mahayanism and *deva* worship (*ibid.*, pp. 209–10)

(8) Throughout the *Records* references to relic worship, legends, miracles, magic, and exorcism are frequent

(9) Statistics of adherents as given by Hsüan Chwang:[1]

Hinayanists..........	96,000
Mahayanists.........	32,000
Mixed..............	54,500
Total............	182,500

4. I-Tsing (traveled in 671–95 A.D.)

(a) I-Tsing distinguishes four main schools of Buddhism in the India of his day

(1) Aryamahasanghikanikaya (or "Noble School of the Great Brotherhood"), seven subdivisions

[1] See Eliot, II, 100, and Rhys Davids, *Journal of the Royal Asiatic Society*, 1891, pp. 418 ff.

(2) Aryasthaviranikaya (or "Noble School of the Elders"), three subdivisions
(3) Aryamulasarvastivadanikaya (or "Noble Fundamental School Which Affirms the Existence of All Things"), four subdivisions
(4) Aryasammitinikaya (or "Noble School of the Right Measure"), four subdivisions (see I-Tsing, [Takakusu's trans.], pp. 7–8)

(*b*) Both Hinayana and Mahayana seemed to be recognized as alternative forms of religion (Eliot, II, 103)

(*b*) I-Tsing notices a decline in the religion within his own day (*ibid.*, p. 103)

(*d*) Most of I-Tsing's narrative is a description of temple and monastic life which does not extend the picture of Buddhism as a whole beyond what Hsüan Chwang tells

X. Decline of Indian Buddhism and Its Submergence in Hinduism

a) References

Barth, Auguste: *The Religions of India*, pp. 133–39. (By one of the older authorities.)

Beal, S: *Buddhist Records of the Western World*

Eliot, Sir Charles: *Hinduism and Buddhism*, II, 107–31. (Probably the best recent treatment in English.)

ERE. Article on "Tantrism," by De la Vallée-Poussin.

Farquhar, J. N.: *An Outline of the Religious Literature of India*, pp. 209–13, 272–74. (For the literature of Tantrik Buddhism.)

Haraprasada, Sastri: "Buddhism in Bengal since the Muhammadan Conquest," *Journal of the Asiatic Society of Bengal*, 1896.

Imperial Gazetteer of India, I, 412–13. (Contains a brief summary statement.)

Nariman, G. K.: *Literary History of Sanskrit Buddhism*, pp. 110–22. (Good discussion of the literature of late Buddhism.)

Oltramare, Paul: *L'histoire des idées théosophiques dans L'Inde*, pp. 495–520. (Seeks to show that Buddhism is a product of Hinduism and remained Hindu in all stages of its career.)

Monier-Williams, Sir Monier: *Buddhism*, pp. 162–71.

Radhakrishnan, S.: *Indian Philosophy*, I, 605–10.

Subrahmanya, Aiyar K. V.: "Origin and Decline of Buddhism and Jainism in Southern India," *Indian Antiquary*, 1911.

Taranatha: *Geschichte des Buddhismus in Indien.* A German translation by Anton Schiefner, of a sixteenth-century history of Buddhism. (An important source but not to be accepted uncritically. From p. 257 on it deals with later Buddhism.)

Vallée-Poussin, L. de la: *Bouddhisme*, pp. 343–412. (A good discussion of every aspect.)

Waddell, Lawrence Austin: *The Buddhism of Tibet or Lamaism*, pp. 5–17. (Gives a vivid brief account of the changes through which Buddhism passed on the way to its late Tantrik phase. By an authority on Tibetan Buddhism.)

Waddell, Lawrence Austin: "The Indian Buddhist Cult of Avalokita and His Consort Tara 'the Saviouress,' Illustrated from the Remains in Magadha," *Journal of the Royal Asiatic Society*, 1894, pp. 51–89.

b) Outline of main points

1. The decay of Buddhism

   (*a*) Had already begun in Hsüan Chwang's time (see above Topic IX)

      (1) He mentions incidentally the worship of the goddess Tara at certain Buddhist shrines (Beal, *Records*, II, 103, 174)

   (*b*) In the eleventh century Buddhism still held power in outlying provinces like Kashmir and Orissa, and the Pal kings of Bihar remained true to the faith until the conquest of the province by Bakhtiyar Khilji in 1193 A.D.

(c) With the establishment of the Moslim power Buddhism disappeared from North India (i.e., in its old home)

(d) In Western India it survived until the middle of the twelfth century when the Saiva revival was directed against both Buddhists and Jains

(1) This does not mean violent persecution but rather a submergence in a rising tide of Hinduism (see Monier-Williams, p. 170, and Eliot, II, 110)

(e) Buddhism in India at the present time (*Imperial Gazetteer of India*, I, 413)

(1) About 300,000 Buddhists scattered in small numbers

(a) Along north and northwest frontiers of Bengal

(b) In the Punjab districts of Spiti, Lahul, and Kanawar

(c) On the lower slope of the Himalayas

(d) In Nepal, though opposed by the Hindu ruling dynasty

(2) In all of these the form is corrupt

2. The character of decadent Buddhism

(a) It became mixed with baser elements from Hinduism

(1) Saktism

(a) The worship of a goddess, or goddesses, as divine energy

(1) In Hinduism this is the worship of Siva's consort (Devi, Durga, Kali, etc.)

(2) In Buddhism it is chiefly the worship of Tara, the consort of Avalokita

(b) It is essentially an erotic mysticism

(2) Tantrism

(a) A system of magical or sacramental ritual which professes to attain the highest aims of religion by

(1) Spells, diagrams, gestures, and other physical exercises (Eliot, II, 274)

(*b*) It produced a literature called *Tantras*, which probably dates from the ninth to the eleventh century (see article on "Buddhist Literature" in *ERE*, Vol. VIII)

(1) These are treatises partly concerned with

(*a*) Ritual (*Kriyatantra*)

(*b*) Rules of conduct (*Charyatantra*)

(*c*) Yogi esotericism (*Yogatantra*)

(1) This starts from the mysticism of the Madhyamaka and the Yogacarya schools

(2) Its teachings are a mixture of mysticism, sorcery, and erotics, accompanied by disgusting rites

(3) In this Buddhism becomes indistinguishable from Saivism

(2) The best-known Buddhist Tantrik work is the *Tathagata Guhaka* (see Farquhar, p. 211)

3. Causes assigned for the disappearance of Buddhism in India

(*a*) Buddhism was always extremely tolerant from the very beginning

(1) Buddha did not prohibit the laity from practicing the customary rites of the general community in matters of birth, death, and marriage (Eliot, II, 120)

(2) While Buddha taught salvation through personal effort in accordance with insight into the four noble truths and not in dependence upon any god, he neither denied the existence of the Hindu gods nor sought to prevent their worship

(*b*) Among the monks Buddhism remained distinct and pure so long as the strict observances of the Hinayana continued (see Barth, cited above, and Poussin, pp. 410–11)

(*c*) But the Mahayana opened the door to Hindu influence even among the monks

(1) By its development of a pantheon of Buddhas and Bodhisattvas
(2) By its development of a metaphysics of a pantheistic world-soul that approaches the Vedanta teaching
(3) By its larger use of the practice of Yoga or ecstatic meditation

(*d*) Buddhism, arising as a variation out of Hinduism, was reabsorbed by it, as Hinduism was the older, stronger current of religious thought and feeling
(1) Hinduism acted by a strong, though slow, assimilative social influence from the fourth century onward (see Eliot, I, xxxiii–xl)

4. Buddhism left its mark, however, upon Hinduism (see Radhakrishnan's remarks on this point [I, 608–10])

PART II

IN CEYLON: CONSERVATION OF THE HINAYANA

I. The Introduction of Buddhism into Ceylon

a) References

Cave, Henry W.: *The Book of Ceylon*, pp. 525–47. From an attractive traveler's guide. Maps and 756 photographs. (The passage cited weaves history and archaeological description together instructively.)

Copleston, R. S.: *Buddhism, Primitive and Present, in Magadha and in Ceylon.* (Pp. 177–95 describe the conversion of Ceylon and contain also a translation of Mahinda's first discourse to King Tissa.)

Eliot, Sir Charles: *Hinduism and Buddhism*, III, 11–17. (Careful, judicious sifting of the materials for the historic facts.)

Hackmann, H.: *Buddhism as a Religion*, pp. 64–67. (Condensed statement of the essentials.)

Mahavamsa, or the Great Chronicle of Ceylon, pp. 82–141. Translated by Geiger in the "Pali Text Society Series." (The most important source. Should be read for the quaint charm of the old legendary accounts and its Buddhistic feeling.)

Mitton, G. E.: *The Lost Cities of Ceylon.* (Chaps. iii and x give a description of Anuradhapura and Mihintale as they appear today. Maps and illustrations.)

Rhys Davids, T. W.: Article on "Ceylon Buddhism" in *ERE*, Vol. III. (Good, succinct, scholarly statement of the whole subject.)

Saunders, Kenneth J.: *Epochs in Buddhist History*, pp. 105–7. (A brief but impressive picture.)

b) Outline

1. The civilization of Ceylon is derived from India

(*a*) Sinhalese art, religion, and language show the influence of both Southern (Tamil) and Northern India, but the latter is stronger

(*b*) The Buddhism of Ceylon is founded upon and has preserved the doctrines and the scriptures current in Magadha at the time of Asoka. The causes for this seem to be (Eliot, III, 12)

(1) Lack of theological originality among the Sinhalese which would inspire modification of doctrine

(2) The chiefs claimed to have come from North India and were loyal to the religion of the same origin

(3) Buddhism acquired stability because it was maintained as national and patriotic as against the faith of the Tamils who were constantly trying to gain a foothold on the island

2. Tradition says that North Indian influence began with the expedition of Vijaya, who with seven hundred followers settled in Ceylon about the time of Buddha's death

(*a*) But there is no clear indication of Buddhism in Ceylon before Asoka's time (Copleston, p. 179)

(*b*) The legends of Buddha's visits to Ceylon are inventions (Eliot says for the purpose of glorifying the island)

3. The books of the Sinhalese tradition (see Eliot, III, 14)

(*a*) The *Dipavamsa*, or "Short Chronicle"; written between 302 and 430 A.D.

(*b*) The *Mahavamsa*, or "Great Chronicle"; written toward the end of the fifth century by Mahanama

(*c*) The Historical Introduction to the *Samantapasadika* by Buddhaghosa

(*d*) All three of the foregoing are based upon an older source, the *Atthakatha*, now lost (see Geiger's Introduction to his translation of the *Mahavamsa*, pp. x–xii)

4. How Buddhism came to Ceylon as recorded in the foregoing three works

(*a*) Tissa's first mission to King Asoka

(1) When Devanampiya Tissa became king of Ceylon,

having great admiration for Asoka, he sent a mission bearing many rich gifts for the latter (*ca.* 245 B.C.)

(2) Asoka responded with many return presents, the information that he had taken refuge in the law of Buddha, and the advice that Tissa do the same

(*b*) The inclusion of Ceylon in Asoka's missionary projects

(1) After the Council of Pataliputra (see above, pp. 17f.), Moggaliputta, who had presided over it, came to the conclusion that the time had come to dispatch missionaries to convert foreign countries (inscriptions imply that Asoka himself initiated the movement; see Smith's *Asoka* for the text of Rock Edict XIII, pp. 172–75)

(2) Mahinda, near-relative of the king, was selected and sent as apostle

(*a*) "The legend tells how Mahinda and his following alighted on the Missaka mountain, whither King Devanampiya Tissa had gone in the course of a hunt. The monk and the royal *cortège* met: Mahinda, after testing the king's intellectual capacity [see *Mahavamsa*, pp. 92–93] by some curious dialectical puzzles, had no difficulty in converting him. Next morning he proceeded to Anuradhapura and was received with all honor and enthusiasm. He preached first in the palace and then to enthusiastic audiences of the general public. In these discourses he dwelt chiefly on the terrible punishment awaiting sinners in future existences" (Eliot, III, 16).

(3) The conversion of the capital

(*a*) Tissa then made a gift to the monks of his own pleasure garden, the Mahamega. (See pictures in Cave, pp. 536–37)

(*b*) Then followed the erection of a number of

religious edifices in the district of Anuradhapura and Mihintale

(1) The greatest of these was the Mahavihara or "Great Monastery," the stronghold of orthodoxy, conserver of the Pali pitakas as we know them

(*c*) Tissa's further missions to India

(1) One was to secure relics, over which when obtained was built the Thuparama Dagoba (see Cave, pp. 538–40)

(2) Another was to bring a branch of the Bo-tree

(*a*) This branch was planted at Anuradhapura and the tree is still exhibited in Mahamegha garden (*ibid.*, pp. 542–45)

(*b*) The *Mahavamsa* says that this mission also brought back Mahinda's sister, a nun, to ordain the Ceylonese ladies wishing to become nuns; her name was Sanghamitta

(*c*) Concerning the tree, Eliot remarks that "botanists consider its long life, though remarkable, not impossible since roots of this species throw up fresh shoots from the roots near the parent stem" (III, 17)

(*d*) Mahinda and the Pali canon

(1) The *Mahavamsa* does not mention books brought by Mahinda to Ceylon

(2) It says that the sacred literature was committed to writing under the reign of Vattagamani, or about one hundred and seventy-five years after Mahinda's death (*Mahavamsa*, p. 237)

(3) Evidently, then, Mahinda brought the Buddhist teachings in his own memory to Ceylon and taught them orally to the monks of the Mahavihara

(4) It was what these monks in turn remembered and passed on that was finally committed to writing and constitutes our Pali texts as we have them today

(e) Significance of the introduction of Buddhism into Ceylon
  (1) The civilization of Ceylon dates from that period
    (a) Architecture, painting, sculpture, all bear the marks of Buddhist influence
    (b) None of the surviving art relics antedates the Buddhist period
      (1) Cave calls Buddhism the "efficient cause of all the constructive energy which the Sinhalese displayed in the erection of their vast cities and monuments" (p. 526)
  (2) The Hinayana Buddhism of Asoka's time was brought into an environment suitable to preserve it unchanged

5. Chief events in Ceylon Buddhist history between the time of Mahinda and that of Buddhaghosa (see Copleston, pp. 196–99, and Eliot, III, 17–28)
  (a) In the reign of Dutthagamani, 101–77 B.C., according to Geiger
    (1) Lohapasada, or the Copper Palace, was built; a meeting place for the monks (Cave, pp. 548–50; *Mahavamsa*, pp. 182–86)
    (2) An immense relic shrine, the Ruwanweli Dagoba was erected (Cave, pp. 550–61; *Mahavamsa*, pp. 187–219)
  (b) In the reign of Vattagamani Abhaya, 29–17 B.C.
    (1) A new monastery and *dagoba*, known as the Abhayagiri, was built
      (a) This soon became an enemy of the Mahavihara, and heterodox
      (b) This schism was apparently the cause for committing the pitakas to writing (*Mahavamsa*, pp. 236–37)
  (c) In the reign of Mahasena, 325–52 A.D.
    (1) The monks of the Abhayagiri were favored and those of the Mahavihara proscribed, while their

buildings were torn down and the materials transferred to the Abhayagiri

(2) Mahasena was later persuaded by his ministers to restore them (for the whole story see *Mahavamsa*, pp. 267–71)

(*d*) In the early part of the fourth century

(1) The use of an image of Mahinda in the religious processions of the Mahavihara began

(2) The Cult of the Sacred Tooth of Buddha arose (see Eliot, III, 22–28; Cave, pp. 307–12; and *Asia*, September, 1927, for picture of procession of the Sacred Tooth)

II. Buddhaghosa, Great Systematizer of the Hinayana

a) References

Buddhaghosuppatti. Translated by James Gray (1892). (A late legendary life of Buddhaghosa written by a Burmese in the sixteenth century A.D. Interesting as showing the impression made by the personality of Buddhaghosa.)

Copleston, R. S.: *Buddhism, Primitive and Present in Magadha and in Ceylon*, pp. 201–18. (Describes the commentarial work of Buddhaghosa and recounts his life.)

Dhammakitti: A Supplementary Passage in the "Mahavamsa," Written in the 13th Century A.D. (Not contained in Geiger's translation. See latter part of chap. xxxvii in Law's *Buddhaghosa*, as listed below, pp. 3–8.)

Eliot, Sir Charles: *Hinduism and Buddhism*, III, 28–32.

Law, Bimala Charon: *The Life and Works of Buddhaghosa* (1923). (Probably the fullest compendium of all that is now known about the man and his work.)

Rhys Davids, Mrs. C. A. F.: *Buddhist Psychology* (1914). (Based upon Buddhaghosa's expositions.)

Rhys Davids, T. W.: Article on "Buddhaghosa" in *ERE*, Vol. II.

Saunders, Kenneth J.: *Epochs in Buddhist History*, pp. 108–11.

Warren, H. C.: *Buddhism in Translations.* (Contains many passages from Buddhaghosa.)

For more extended examples of Buddhaghosa's work see the following translations in the "Pali Text Society Series": Nos. 8 and 9: *The Expositor* (being a translation in two volumes of the *Atthasalini*, a commentary on one of the Abhidhamma works on mental elements or processes); No. 11: *The Path of Purity* (being a translation of Part I on "Virtue [or Morals] of Visuddhimagga," Buddhaghosa's monumental summary of Buddhist doctrine).

b) Outline

1. Sources for the life of Buddhaghosa
   (*a*) Scattered biographical references in his writings
      (1) Law utilizes many of these in chap. i of his work
   (*b*) Dhammakitti's continuation of the *Mahavamsa* (see above)
   (*c*) *Buddhaghosuppatti:* a Pali work by Mahamangala (see above)
2. Essential facts concerning his life
   (*a*) Born into a Brahman family in India, he first lived the life of a wandering disputant
   (*b*) He was converted to Buddhism through the influence of a monk named Revata
   (*c*) Showed an interest in Buddhist doctrine by composing
      (1) A treatise entitled *Jananodaya* ("Uprising of Knowledge")
      (2) An essay entitled *Atthasalini* ("Full of Meaning")
         (*a*) This was probably the groundwork for the commentary later produced in Ceylon (see Law, pp. 69–70)
   (*d*) Revata, seeing that he contemplated writing commentaries on the pitaka, advised him to go to Ceylon where the ancient commentaries were still known, the texts alone being extant in India, and to translate the commentaries into Pali
   (*e*) Buddhaghosa arrived in Ceylon in the reign of Maha-

nama, who ruled from 458 to 480 A.D. according to Geiger (*Mahav.*, p. xxxix)

(*f*) After having studied under Sanghapali at the Mahavihara he asked permission to translate the commentaries

(1) The monks wishing proof of his competence for the task, he composed the celebrated *Visuddhimagga*

(*g*) Then in the seclusion of the Ganthakara Vihara he translated the commentaries into Pali, after which he returned to India

3. The legendary account of the *Buddhaghosuppatti*

(*a*) An ornate retelling of Dhammakitti's account with an apparent application to Buddhaghosa of stories concerning other individuals told elsewhere in the *Milinda Panha Dialog* and earlier parts of the *Mahavamsa* (see Law, pp. 44–47)

4. The works of Buddhaghosa (after *ibid.*, pp. 68–94)

(*a*) The *Visuddhimagga*

(1) An encyclopedic exposition of the whole system of Pali Buddhism

(2) For its influence in Ceylon see Saunders, pp. 108–9

(*b*) Commentaries on the Tipitaka

(1) On the Vinaya Pitaka

(*a*) The *Samantapasadika:* "This work itself," says Law, "supplies us with sufficient materials with which to write a social, political, moral, religious and philosophical history of Ancient India."

(*b*) The *Kankhavitarani:* a commentary on the Patimokkha

(2) On the Sutta Pitaka

(*a*) The *Sumangalavilasini:* gives a "vivid picture of sports and pastimes, geographical position of countries, effects of the life of a recluse etc., in ancient days." On Digha-nikaya (long discourses) (*b*) The *Papancasudani:* a commentary on the Majjhima Nikaya

(*c*) The *Saratthapakasini:* a commentary on the Samyutta Nikaya, which itself consists of five series of works

(*d*) The *Manorathapurani:* a commentary on the Anguttara Nikaya, which is divided into eleven parts

(*e*) The *Khuddaka-nikayatthakatha:* commentaries on certain books of the Khuddaka-nikaya (or short discourses)

(3) On the Abhidhamma Pitaka

(*a*) The *Atthasalini:* a commentary on the Dhammasangani (or enumeration of *dhammas*, i.e., mental elements)

(*b*) *Sammohavinodani:* a commentary on the Vibhanga (another work of psychological analysis)

(*c*) *Dhatukathapakaranatthakatha:* on the Dhatukatha (or "Discussion of Elements")

(*d*) *Puggala pannattipakaranatthakatha:* on the Puggala Pannatti (or "Description of Individuals," i.e., according to their stages along the path)

(*e*) *Kathavatthu atthakatha:* on the Kathavatthu (or "Points of Controversy")

(*f*) *Yamakapakaranatthakatha:* on the Yamaka (or "Book of Pairs." "The subject matter is psychology and the analysis is arranged as pairs of questions."—THOMAS, *Life of Buddha*, p. 277)

(*g*) *Patthanapakaranatthakatha:* on the Patthana (or "Book of Relations." Treats of causality, etc.)

(*c*) Certain other works about which little is known or about whose authorship there is doubt (see Law, pp. 85–92)

NOTE.—For classification and brief description of each of the works in the Pali canon as known to Buddhaghosa the reader will find Thomas' *Life of Buddha as Legend and History*, pp. 257–77, a most convenient reference.

5. Despite his tremendous industry Buddhaghosa did not complete commentaries on the entire Pali canon
   (*a*) Other lesser but noteworthy scholars finished the task (for these see Law, pp. 95–103)
      (1) Buddhadatta
      (2) Dhammapala
      (3) Mahanama
      (4) Moggallana
      (5) Cullabuddhaghosa
6. The value of Buddhaghosa's contribution
   (*a*) Was not in originality of thought
   (*b*) But in his faithful adherence to the authorities of the old Buddhism
   (*c*) And in his ordering of the materials of the Hinayana teaching in the form that has been authoritative for that branch of Buddhism ever since
      (1) He may not improperly be called the St. Thomas of Hinayana scholasticism
   (*d*) His efforts crowned the conserving work of the Buddhists of Ceylon by means of which we are able to make our nearest approach to the origin of Buddhism itself

III. BUDDHISM IN CEYLON AT THE PRESENT DAY

a) References

Buddhist Annual of Ceylon. Published in Colombo by W. E. Bastian. (Interesting as revealing the activities of certain Westerners in promoting Buddhism.)

Copleston: *Buddhism, Primitive and Present, in Magadha and in Ceylon* (2d ed., 1908), pp. 242–87. (The fullest single reference on the topic.)

Dharmapala, Anagarika: "On the Eightfold Path," *Asia*, September, 1927. (By a modern Sinhalese Buddhist influenced by theosophy.)

Eliot, Sir Charles: *Hinduism and Buddhism*, III, 41–44.

Gogerly, D. J.: *Ceylon Buddhism*, I, 1–14. (Written in 1865 by a scholarly observer. Contains some references to certain modern practices in contrast to the ancient teachings.)

Hackmann, H.: *Buddhism as a Religion*, pp. 96–126. (Good statement of monastic practices and organization.)

Hardy, Spence: *Eastern Monachism* (1850), pp. 309–30. (Describes the priesthood as it appeared to an observer nearly a century ago.)

Saunders, Kenneth J.: *The Story of Buddhism* (1916), pp. 76–98. (As seen by a sympathetic modern observer.)

Saunders, Kenneth J.: *Buddhism and Buddhists in Southern Asia* (1923), pp. 24–36. (Describes the types of Buddhist influence in modern Ceylon, and considers them in relation to Christian influence.)

b) Outline

1. The teaching
   (*a*) The moral system is still that of the sacred books, whether taught by the traditional or the reforming parties
   (*b*) But the history and cosmogony that have been handed down belong to late Buddhist tradition
      (1) Jataka tales, many universes, heavens, and hells, world-cycles, etc.
      (2) This element tends to dissolve in the minds of Sinhalese with modern education
2. The monastic life (see Hackmann and Copleston)
   (*a*) Entrance into the order
      (1) Children destined for the priesthood go through a period of tutelage from the age of eight to eleven or twelve
         (*a*) Each under a particular monk with whom the parents make arrangement
      (2) From twelve to twenty: the novitiate
         (*a*) Enters by a simple ceremony called "Pabbaja" in which the hair is cut and the robes taken
         (*b*) The novice memorizes certain books, follows

prescribed rules as to daily living, and waits upon his tutor (see Copleston, pp. 268–69, and Hackmann, pp. 98–99)

(3) At the age of twenty is admitted to full monkhood in a ceremony called "Upasampada"

(*a*) This ceremony, which is held annually, is performed as a rule only at two monasteries in Kandy, Malwatte and Asgiri, which have a prominent position

(*b*) Entrance into monkhood is not binding for lifetime

(*c*) Life and character of the monks

(1) Daily duties

(*a*) Certain domestic work

(*b*) Reading and learning the sacred text

(*c*) Meditation

(*d*) Devotion before the images

(*e*) Begging for food (Copleston, p. 264)

(1) This food is not necessarily eaten by the priests

(2) Other activities

(*a*) Instruction of children

(1) Desultory (see Saunders, *Buddhism in Southern Asia*, p. 28).

(2) Limited in content to the sacred books

(*b*) Healing of sickness by use of charms and chants (Saunders, *Story of Buddhism*, pp. 82–84)

(*c*) Public recitation of sacred texts

(1) This may be at a gathering of village folk (Copleston, pp. 257–59; Saunders, *Buddhism in Southern Asia*, pp. 26–28)

(2) Or at the temple on *poya* days (i.e., on the four quarters of the moon) (Copleston, pp. 259–60)

(3) The general level of the intellectual and moral life of the priesthood is not high (Hackmann, pp. 116–18; Copleston, p. 269)

3. The Buddhism of the laity
   (*a*) Among the peasants it is mixed with demon worship and in some places Hinduism (Eliot, III, 42; Copleston, pp. 272–75)
      (1) The monks recite certain sacred texts in a ceremony called "Pirit" to ward off the influences of malignant spirits (Gogerly, I, 5; Saunders, *Story of Buddhism*, p. 83)
   (*b*) Among modern educated Sinhalese, Buddhism appeals because (see *Buddhism in Southern Asia*, pp. 31–32)
      (1) It is associated with the greatness of Ceylon's past and therefore a factor in the spirit of nationalism (Dharmapala's article illustrates this)
      (2) Its moral standards, uncovered afresh by modern Western scholarship, have value in themselves
      (3) It has found protagonists among certain Westerners who advocate the propagation of Buddhism in the West (for example see any number of the *Buddhist Annual of Ceylon*, also Dharmapala's article in *Asia*)
   (*c*) Questions concerning the modern Buddhist revival in Ceylon
      (1) How far is it a real outgrowth of the old Buddhist stock?
      (2) How far is it a foreign importation?

PART III

IN CHINA: MAHAYANA IN ITS FULL DEVELOPMENT

I. The Introduction and General History of Buddhism in China

a) References

Note.—Any of the writers that deal with Chinese Buddhism treat to some extent of this topic, but the references which present most accurately the present state of our knowledge of the subject are the ones given.

Bose, Phanindranath: *The Indian Teachers in China* (1923). (An excellent compilation and organization of available facts concerning the Indian Buddhist missionaries to China.)

Eliot, Sir Charles: *Hinduism and Buddhism*, III, 244–80. (Most comprehensive English account.)

Groot, J. J. M. de: *Sectarianism and Religious Persecution in China* (1903). 2 vols. (Based largely on imperial decrees, the texts and translations of which are given. See the Index for passages on Buddhism.)

Hodous, Lewis: *Buddhism and Buddhists in China* (1924), pp. 4–6. (A brief statement of the essentials regarding the entrance of Buddhism into China. A suggestive division of the periods of Buddhist history in China will be found on p. 63.)

Maspero, M. H.: "Le songe et l'ambassade de l'Empereur Ming: Critique des sources," *Bulletin de l'Ecole Française d'Extrême Orient*, X (1910), 95–130. (A basic study of the traditional legend concerning the introduction of Buddhism into China.)

Moore, George Foot: *History of Religions*, I, 79–92. (Very brief treatment of historical along with other phases of Chinese Buddhism.)

Reichelt, K. L.: *Truth and Tradition in Chinese Buddhism*

(1927), 9.25. (A rather cursory, interpretative account by a very sympathetic student of the Mahayana.)

Wieger, Leon: *Bouddhisme chinois*, I (1910), 108–10. (Brief historical outline which accepts the traditional date for the entrance of Buddhism into China, by a Jesuit sinologue of note.)

Wieger, Leon: *Histoire des croyances religieuses et des opinions philosophiques en Chine* (1917), p. 355.

b) Outline

1. Traditional story of the introduction of Buddhism into China: The Emperor Ming (ruled 58–75 A.D.) of the eastern Han dynasty, having seen Buddha in a dream, sent ambassadors to India to inquire into his doctrine; on their return these ambassadors brought the holy books and statues as well as two Indian monks, who commenced to translate the Buddhist writings into Chinese. The embassy returned about 67 A.D., so the dream would have been a few years earlier.
   (*a*) The chief criticism of the story is that before 73 A.D. Central Asia was in rebellion against China and not a likely place for such an envoy to travel through, though the only route
   (*b*) Eliot's reply to the criticism is that to send envoys to inquire about religion may have been politically advantageous and so not in itself improbable
2. There are evidences, however, of earlier Buddhist contacts
   (*a*) The interpretation of the dream implies prior knowledge of Buddhism
   (*b*) Documents discovered by Stein on the western frontier of Kansu prove that China had communication with Central Asia earlier; Buddhism was therefore not likely to escape notice
   (*c*) In 121 B.C. the *Annals* relate that "a golden man" was captured from the Hsiung-nu
   (*d*) Still earlier tradition relates that an ambassador of Wu-Ti visited Central Asia where he learned something of

the new religion and brought back an account of Buddha's golden statue

(*e*) The *Wei-lüeh* states that in the year 2 B.C. an ambassador of the Emperor Ai to the court of the Yüeh Chih was instructed in Buddhism by order of their king

(*f*) Later *Han Annals* intimate that in 65 A.D. the Prince of Ch'u was a Buddhist and that there were Sramanas and Upasakas in his territory

(*g*) The policy of the Chinese government of moving conquered peoples into China proper would naturally bring their religion with them (see Hodous, p. 5)

3. Religious conditions which prepared the way for the spread of Buddhism in China

   (*a*) Confucianism had become official and burdensome (see Hodous, p. 5, and Reichelt, p. 9)

   (*b*) Taoism had become corrupt in its practice and brought about a reaction of the purists who sought to return to the earlier Taoist mysticism (Hodous, pp. 9–10); these latter recognized a kinship between Taoist and Buddhist aspirations as well as the superiority of Buddhist forms of worship

4. Buddhism as first introduced by the two monks Kasyapa Matanga and Gobharana (after Wieger, *Histoire des croyances religieuses et des opinions philosophiques en Chine*, p. 355)

   (*a*) Works produced for the emperor

      (1) A résumé of the legends on the birth and infancy of Buddha

      (2) A summary of his preaching.

      (3) A short exposition of Buddhist principles

         (*a*) This was the sutra of 42 sections which alone survived of these early works

         (*b*) It is essentially Hinayanistic

      (4) A résumé of the ascetic way to be followed by aspirants after perfection

   (*b*) The teachings of the first two missionaries (according

to Chinese annals)
- (1) The sanctity of all animal life
- (2) Metempsychosis
- (3) Meditation
- (4) Asceticism
- (5) *Karma*

5. The fortunes of Buddhism through the dynasties (after Eliot)
   - (*a*) During the later Han dynasty, 25–221 A.D.
     - (1) Three hundred and fifty works were translated into Chinese by twelve different Indian monks, half of whom were from India and half from Central Asia
   - (*b*) During the three kingdoms, 221–65 A.D.
     - (1) The translation of the *Patimokkha* indicates growth of monastic life
     - (2) The presence of five translators at Nanking indicates the southward spread of the religion
     - (3) Other translators were at work in Loyang
   - (*c*) Dynasty of western Tsin, 265–316 A.D.
     - (1) Buddhism begins to become prominent
   - (*d*) Later Chao, *ca.* 273–375 (in North China)
     - (1) Under Tartar rule Buddhism was favored
     - (2) General permission given the populace to enter monasteries
     - (3) By 381 A.D. nine-tenths of the inhabitants of Northwestern China were said to be Buddhists
     - (4) By 372 A.D. Buddhism had been introduced into Korea
   - (*e*) Former Ts'in, 351–94 A.D.
     - (1) The connections with western regions were close
   - (*f*) Later Ts'in, 384–417 A.D.
     - (1) Kumarajiva, the greatest of the Indian translators of the early period (see Bose, pp. 51–73)
       - (*a*) Patronized by the emperor
       - (*b*) Said to have had three thousand disciples
       - (*c*) Fifty extant translations are ascribed to him

(*g*) Eastern Ts'in; at Nanking from 317 to 420 A.D.
- (1) Buddhism was favored and the ninth sovereign, Hsiao Wu-Ti, was the first Chinese emperor to become a Buddhist

(*h*) Liu Sung dynasty, 420–80 A.D. (in the south)
- (1) There were indications that Buddhism was flourishing
- (2) But also the beginnings of restrictive legislation by the official class
  - (*a*) The emperor was asked to prevent the multiplication of monasteries and expenditures in superstitious ceremonies
- (3) There were twenty translators, partly native and partly foreigners, from Central Asia, India, and Ceylon
- (4) Twenty-five Chinese started on a pilgrimage to India in 420 A.D.
  - (*a*) Fa Hsien had traveled from 399 to 414 (see above, pp. 32 f.)

(*i*) Wei dynasty (contemporaneous with Liu Sung)
- (1) Buddhism was persecuted by one emperor who decreed that all images and sacred books should be destroyed and all priests executed (De Groot, I, 28–32)
- (2) But his successors tolerated and even promoted it

(*j*) Liang dynasty, 502–57 A.D.
- (1) Buddhism prospered greatly under imperial patronage and popular approval
  - (*a*) The first edition of the Chinese Tripitaka was collected in manuscript in 518 A.D.
  - (*b*) In 520 or 525 A.D. Bodhidharma, reputed founder of the Meditative School in China, arrived from India

(*k*) From the end of the Liang dynasty to the beginning of the T'ang, 557–620 A.D.

(1) Some persecution of Buddhism along with Taoism, but Buddhism prospered on the whole

(*l*) T'ang dynasty, 620–907 A.D.

(1) A period of struggle between Confucianism, Buddhism, and Taoism

(*a*) The emperors and the Confucian court were often hostile to Buddhism though some favored it; some emperors persecuted Buddhists in the early part of their reign and promoted it in later life

(2) Hsüan Chuang traveled to India (629–45 A.D.) (see above, pp. 33 f.), and was fortunate to return under a favorable emperor

(3) Buddhism suffered its greatest persecution under Wu Tsung in 845 A.D. who was instigated by Taoists (for details see De Groot, I, 59–69)

(*m*) Sung dynasty, 960–1280 A.D.

(1) A great period of Chinese art largely inspired by Buddhism

(2) Literature and philosophy were likewise influenced

(*a*) Chu Hsi and his masters show this

(*b*) Also Lu Chiu-yüan, who taught knowledge through meditation

(*n*) The Yüan or Mongol dynasty, 1280–1368 A.D.

(1) Buddhism was consistently favored

(2) The form most favored was Lamaism, one of the temples of which has been maintained in Peking ever since

(*o*) Ming dynasty, 1368–1644 A.D.

(1) Though Confucianism was in the ascendance Buddhism was treated with respect

(2) The early Catholic missionaries found Buddhism their chief rival

(*p*) Manchu dynasty, 1644–1911 A.D.

(1) Considerable attention was paid by the throne to representatives of Tibetan Buddhism, possibly for reasons more political than religious

(2) The twelfth and last collection of the Tripitaka under monarchical rule was made

(q) Since the revolution of 1911 (see Hodous, pp. 64–69)

(1) Buddhism shows new signs of revival, propaganda, and reform

II. Bodhidharma and Chih-K'ai: The Foundation of the Meditative and T'ien-T'ai Schools

a) References

Eliot, Sir Charles: *Hinduism and Buddhism*, pp. 304–12.

Hackmann, H.: *Buddhism as a Religion*, pp. 238–41. (A very summary account.)

Johnston, R. F.: *Buddhist China*, pp. 82–90. (By an intimate student of Chinese Buddhism.)

Reichelt, Karl L.: *Truth and Tradition in Chinese Buddhism*, pp. 45–56. (Good statement of the essentials.)

Saunders, Kenneth J.: *Epochs in Buddhist History*, pp. 134–50. (An impressive description, with attention to Japanese interpretations.)

Wieger, Leon: *Histoire des croyances religieuses et des opinions philosophiques en Chine*, pp. 519–28. (Holds that the followers of the "Meditative" school are essentially Vedantists.)

b) Outline

1. Schools of Chinese Buddhism

(a) The names of ten are listed by Hackmann (p. 238)

(b) Distinctions have been long since obliterated, however, and the most important for present-day study are

(1) Ch'an (or "Contemplative") school

(2) The T'ien-T'ai school

(3) The "Pure Land" school

2. The Contemplative (or Meditative) school

(a) Founded by Bodhidharma who came to China from India in 520 (or 526) A.D.

(1) Bodhidharma is accounted the twenty-eighth patriarch in the line of direct descent from Sakyamuni (Reichelt, p. 46)

- (2) He appears, however, to be unknown to both Indian and Tibetan writers (Eliot, p. 306)
- (3) For personal stories concerning Bodhidharma see Saunders, pp. 135–37

(b) The teaching of Bodhidharma

- (1) The only true reality is the Buddha nature in the heart of every man
- (2) All that man needs to do is to turn his gaze inward and see the Buddha in his heart
  - (a) Prayer, asceticism, good works, are vain
- (3) The final vision is an intuition which comes in a moment
  - (a) It cannot be taught or learned
    - (1) Teaching can only prepare the way for it

(c) This teaching resembles certain passages in the Upanishads, and seems almost an anticipation of Sankara's monism

(d) Bodhidharma's teaching harmonized with Taoism and therefore appealed doubtless to a deep-rooted strain in the Chinese character

(e) Successors of Bodhidharma

- (1) Seng-ts'an
- (2) Tao-hsin
- (3) Hui-jen
- (4) Hui-neng (d. 713)

(f) Between the eighth and tenth centuries five subdivisions developed, the most important and dominant of which was the Lin Chi

3. The T'ien-T'ai school

(a) The founder was Chih-K'ai (or Chih-I), who lived in the latter half of the sixth century

- (1) Originally a follower of Bodhidharma, he came to stress the value of study of the scriptures
  - (a) He held that the Buddha mind is present in all living things, but that instruction is necessary to enable them to come to the knowledge and use of it

(b) The T'ien-T'ai school was many sided and inclusive

(1) It approved ecstasy, literature, ceremonial, and discipline

(*c*) Chih-K'ai attempted to harmonize the enormous variety of Buddhist literature by the hypothesis that Buddha set forth progressively different teachings in different periods of his life

(1) During the first three weeks after enlightenment he taught the Hua-yen Ching to heavenly beings

(2) During the next twelve years the Hinayana sutras to his earthly disciples; the Arhat ideal

(3) During the next eight years he taught the peculiarly Mahayana doctrines; the Bodhisattva ideal

(4) During the next twenty-two years of his life, showing that there is no contradiction between Hinayana and Mahayana, he taught the Prajnaparamita sutras

(5) Finally, in old age he taught the deepest, most inclusive doctrine of all, that of the Saddharma Pundarika, or "Lotus Scripture," the crown and summit of all Buddhism

NOTE.—The arbitrariness of this arrangement has been recognized by Japanese scholars (see Saunders, p. 147, and Reichelt, pp. 55 f.).

(*d*) The significance of the T'ien-T'ai school

(1) Its influence spread a remarkable spirit of toleration through Buddhist society (Reichelt, p. 53)

(2) It produced numerous scholars (*ibid.*, p. 55; Eliot, p. 312)

(*e*) For an example of Chih-K'ai's writing see Beal's *Catena of Chinese Scriptures*, pp. 250–73

III. THE FLOWER OF THE MAHAYANA: THE PURE LAND SCHOOL

a) References

Eliot, Sir Charles: *Hinduism and Buddhism*, III, 312–14.

Hackmann, H.: *Buddhism as a Religion*, p. 243.

Johnston, R. F.: *Buddhist China*, pp. 92–121. (A good description of the main characteristics of the Pure Land school as the popular religion of the Buddhist layman.)

Reichelt, K. L.: *Truth and Tradition in Chinese Buddhism*, pp. 127–70. (Valuable for its insight into the religious experience as mediated by the Pure Land school.)

Sukhavati Vyuha Sutras ("The Scriptures of the Pure Land"), in SBE, Vol. XLIX.

Wieger, Leon: *Histoire des croyances et des opinions philosophiques en Chine*, pp. 92–121. (Description of the sect and translations from some of the literature.)

b) Outline

1. The Pure Land is possibly the oldest of all the Mahayana schools
   (*a*) Its idea of deferring one's own Nirvana for the sake of others goes back to the example of Gotama himself (see Wieger, p. 561)
   (*b*) Its principles are traceable to Asvaghosha and Nagarjuna (Reichelt, p. 127)
2. The great leaders of the Pure Land school
   (*a*) Hui-yüan (333–416), who really established the school
      (1) A converted Taoist who used Taoist language to help express the ideas of the school
   (*b*) T'an-luan (502–49 A.D.)
   (*c*) Tao-ch'o (d. 646 A.D.)
   (*d*) Shan-tao (d. 681 A.D.)
      (1) Reichelt thinks he was probably influenced by the conceptions and example of Nestorian Christianity (p. 132)
3. Much of the religious spirit of the school finds expression in the book of common worship, *Ch'an-men Jih-sung* (for description and translations see Reichelt, pp. 134–40)
4. The chief doctrines
   (*a*) Amitabha is the savior of the world
      (1) He is supposed to have attained this position because of a series of vows made ages ago when he was the monk Dharmakara (see Johnston, pp. 96–99)

(b) Salvation is through the invocation of the name of Amitabha with faith
   (1) This has given rise to the prayer so common in the East
      (a) Namo Omito-Fu (in Chinese)
      (b) Namo Amida Butsu (in Japanese)
      (c) Namo Amida Pul (in Korean)
   (2) He who constantly utters this prayer with faith will be reborn at death into the Pure Land, the Western heaven
(c) Other doctrines in common with other schools
   (1) Transmigration
   (2) Recognition of the historical Buddha as the earthly lord and founder of the society

5. Danger of the Pure Land school
   (a) Tendency to exaggerated emphasis upon the efficacy of the mechanical repetition of a name, apart from moral effort
      (1) This has led to a reaction in other schools in the Hinayanistic direction (Reichelt, p. 150)
6. Values of the Pure Land teaching
   (a) It leads to a reliance on faith primarily rather than on works, such as self-discipline, study, asceticism, or meditation
      (1) In this respect it is similar to the psychological discovery of Paul, Augustine, and Luther
   (b) It provides a religion within the understanding and the practice of the common man (see Johnston, pp. 102–7; note the picture of the "Ship of Salvation" opposite p. 104; see also the catechism of the Pure Land in Reichelt, pp. 165–70)

IV. Personalities of the Spiritual World: The Chinese Buddhist Pantheon

a) References

Eliot, Sir Charles: *Hinduism and Buddhism*, Vol. II, chap. xvii. (Deals especially with Bodhisattvas.)

Geden, A. S.: Article on "Images and Idols [Buddhist]" in *ERE*, Vol. VII. (Images in China are treated on pp. 125 f.)

Hackmann, H.: *Buddhism as a Religion*, pp. 206–7. (A brief statement of the essentials.)

Hodous, Lewis: *Buddhism and Buddhists in China.* See pp. 29–33 on "Kwan-Yin" and pp. 51–33 on "Amitabha."

Johnston, R. F.: *Buddhist China.* See pp. 170–206 on "Ti-Tsang" and pp. 259–311 on "Kwan-Yin."

Monier-Williams, Monier: *Buddhism* (1889), pp. 465–92. (A description of the chief characteristics of Buddhist images, based mostly on those of India and Tibet but applicable also to those of China.)

Reichelt, K. L.: *Truth and Tradition in Chinese Buddhism*, pp. 171–202. (Good systematic presentation, with the Chinese characters of the names given.)

Vallée-Poussin, L. de la: Articles on "Avalokitesvara" and "Bodhisattva" in *ERE*, Vol. II. (Discusses the significance of these beings in the light of Sanskrit Mahayana literature.)

Watters, T.: "The Eighteen Lohan of Chinese Buddhism," *Journal of the Royal Asiatic Society*, April, 1899. (By a careful Chinese scholar. On the *arhats* as they are figured in China.)

For pictorial presentation the reader will find the following helpful:

Binyon, Laurence: *Painting in the Far East*, Pls. III, V, VI, XVII.

Fenollosa, E. F.: *Epochs of Chinese and Japanese Art*, I, 86, 122, 132, 134, 142.

Getty, A.: *Gods of Northern Buddhism.* (Good for pictures of Buddhist temple images, though the majority are from Japan.)

Pelliot, Paul: *Les grottes de Touen-Houang.* 7 vols. (Splendid photographs of images and wall paintings in the Tung-Huang caves in West China.)

Perzynski, Friedrich: *Von Chinas Göttern.* (Some excellent plates of images and temples in different parts of China.)

Stein, Mark Aurel: *The Thousand Buddhas; Ancient Buddhist Paintings from the Cave-Temples of Tung-Huang on the Western Frontier of China.* . . . . (with an introductory essay by Laurence Binyon), Vol. I: text; Vol. II: plates. (Exquisite colored plates, fully described, of Chinese Mahayanist paintings of the T'ang period. Buddhas and Bodhisattvas in their heavens.)

Waley, Arthur: *Introduction to Chinese Painting,* Pls. XV, XXI, XXII, XXXI, XXXII.

b) Outline: the classification of the beings of the Chinese Buddhist pantheon (after Reichelt and Hackmann)

1. Buddhas
   (*a*) Shih-chia-mu-ni (the historic Gotama)
   - (1) Generally represented seated in meditation on a lotus blossom, though sometimes he is standing
   - (2) Sometimes figured as the emaciated ascetic
   - (3) Sometimes in a reclining position as entering Nirvana
     - (*a*) This figure the Chinese call the "sleeping Buddha"

   (*b*) The celestial Buddhas
   - (1) O-mi-to-fu (Amitabha)
     - (*a*) Often represented with unusually long arms hanging down
     - (*b*) Sometimes called the "Chieh-yin-fu," or Buddha who receives and guides into paradise
     - (*c*) Called by Reichelt "the figure of the great compassionate All-Father"
   - (2) Yo-shih-fu (Bhaisajyaguru)
     - (*a*) The god of medicine or healing; invoked in sickness
     - (*b*) In the Yo-shih Sutra portrayed as the great source of light
   - (3) P'i-lu-che-na (Vairocana) (see Reichelt, p. 106)

- (*a*) The incarnation of Buddha's "law" or doctrine (*dharma*)
- (*b*) Represented with hands folded over the breast with the forefinger pointing up
- (*c*) Was early connected with the T'ien-T'ai school

(4) Lu-she-na (Lochana) (Reichelt, pp. 106 and 178)

- (*a*) The incarnation of the association or "order" (*sangha*)
- (*b*) Represented with the right hand resting in the lap while the left is raised midway, the tips of the thumb and middle finger touching

(5) Jan-teng-fu (Dipankara); in Western China

- (*a*) Regarded as having once been a human Buddha (see Reichelt, p. 141)
- (*b*) The body is generally covered with lamps which are kept constantly burning, 108 in number

(6) Countless other Buddhas who fill the whole universe

- (*a*) Indicated by innumerable little images in a special hall called "Hall of the 10,000 Buddhas" (note picture in Reichelt, opp. p. 143)

2. Bodhisattvas (Chinese: *p'u-ti-sa-to* or *p'u-sa*), perfected spirits who abstain from participation in eternal blessedness in order to save others from misery (see Johnston, p. 68)

(*a*) Kuan-Yin (Avalokitesvara), the deity who heeds the cry of misery and bends down to the suffering

(1) According to the "Lotus Scripture" the superior of all other Bodhisattvas, and a savior (see Poussin, art. "Avalokitesvara" in *ERE*)

(2) In earlier Indian forms as Avalokitesvara a male figure, but as Kuan-Yin in China and Kwannon in Japan generally represented as female

- (*a*) Causes of this change are obscure (see Eliot, II, 17 f.)

(b) For a Chinese painting of a male Kuan-Yin see Binyon, Pl. III, facing p. 76

(3) Kuan-Yin is the embodiment of motherly tenderness and womanly grace, the "Goddess of Mercy," the Madonna of the Far East (see Johnston, pp. 267–74)

(4) For popular legends concerning Kuan-Yin see Hodous, pp. 30–31; Reichelt, pp. 182–83; Johnston, p. 301

(b) Ta-shih-chih (Mahasthamaprapta)

(1) With Kuan-Yin one of the attendants of Amitabha

(2) In images, Amitabha in the center, Kuan-Yin on the left, and Ta-shih-chi on the right are the "three holy ones of the Western Region" (Hackmann, p. 211)

(3) His most important attribute is power (Reichelt, pp. 185 f.)

(c) Wen-shu (Manjusri)

(1) The Bodhisattva of wisdom (Reichelt, p. 119)

(2) The "Lord of Speech," the "Prince" (Eliot, II, 19)

(3) Represented as riding on a lion (Hackmann, p. 211)

(d) P'u-hsien (Samantabhadra)

(1) The Bodhisattva of grace or mercy (Reichelt, pp. 202, 292)

(2) The patron saint of Mount Omei in China (Eliot, II, 23)

(3) Represented as riding on an elephant (Hackmann, p. 211)

(e) Mi-lo-fu (Maitreya), the future Buddha

(1) The Bodhisattva who awaits in heaven his time to be born as a Buddha (Eliot, II, 21)

(2) In China as a tutelary god represented by a fat, laughing figure at the entrance to temples (Hackmann, p. 209)

(3) The Messiah of Buddhism (Reichelt, pp. 186–88)

(4) Supposed to have made special revelations to Asanga (see Watters, *On Yuan Chwang*, I, 355 f.)

(5) For the history of the idea of Maitreya see N. Peri, *Bulletin de l'Ecole Française d'Extrême-Orient*, 1911, pp. 439–57

(*f*) Ti-ts'ang (Kshitigarbha)

(1) The meaning of his name is "earth-womb" or "earth-treasury"

(*a*) For explanation see Johnston, pp. 170–73

(2) He is called the "savior of the lower world" (Reichelt, p. 100)

(*a*) His function is to rescue suffering spirits from hell

(3) Inconspicuous in the Indian Pantheon, he grew in esteem in Turkestan and gained great importance in the Far East (see Eliot, II, 24, and III, 221)

(4) For his story as told in the Ti-ts'ang *sutra* see Johnston, pp. 175–94, and Reichelt, pp. 119–26

3. Saints (*arhats* or, in Chinese, *lohan*)

(*a*) Buddha's first ten disciples (see Reichelt, p. 189). Of these the images are seldom seen in temples; the most important are

(1) Ananda and Kasyapa

(*a*) These two are sometimes represented on each side of the Buddha Gautama, Ananda as a younger man and Kasyapa as an older one, both in reverential attitude with folded hands (Hackmann, p. 212)

(*b*) The eighteen *lo-han* (Reichelt, p. 191)

(1) Legendary beings with a historical background (Hackmann)

(*a*) For their stories and description see Watters, "The Eighteen Lohan of Chinese Buddhism," in reference above

(b) Sylvain Levi and Ed. Chavannes also discuss them in *Journal asiatique*, 1916

(c) The five hundred *lo-han;* seen in a few large temples

(1) For pictures of some of these see Reichelt, p. 209. For a rather remarkable single *lo-han* see Perzynski, Pls. 43, 44, 45

(2) Hackmann says that in some instances likenesses of K'ang-hsi, Ch'ien-lung, and even Marco Polo have been set among these (p. 212)

(d) Patriarchs

(1) Tamo (Bodhidharma) is chief of these

(a) See Topic II on Bodhidharma and Chih-K'ai above

(2) His five followers come next in the order of their succession

(3) Sometimes certain ones of the Indian patriarchs are added among the images in the Hall of the Patriarchs (see Reichelt, p. 193)

(e) Tutelary deities (Ch'ieh-lan); for details concerning these see Reichelt, pp. 193–97. Their classes are

(1) Twenty four *devas* (Chu-t'ien)

(2) Four heavenly kings (T'ien-wang)

(3) Two guardians at the outside temple door (Heng Ha erh chiang)

(4) Eight guardian angels (Ching-kang Shen)

(5) Four archangels (Ching-kang p'u-sa)

(f) Trinity groups (Reichelt, pp. 197–202)

(1) These are not new figures but triadic groupings of some of the great beings listed above, with various symbolical significance; in this way is found symbolized

(a) The Buddha, the Law, and the Order

(b) The Absolute, its heavenly emanation, and earthly reflex

(c) The Universe in Essence, Image (manifestation); and Action

V. Buddhist Literature in China·

a) References

Bagchi, Prabodh Chandra: *Le canon bouddhique en Chine*, Vol. I: *Les traducteurs et les traductions* (1927). (An inventory of the books according to epochs, including titles of lost as well as of extant works.)

Beal, Samuel: *A Catena of Buddhist Scriptures from the Chinese* (1871). (A series of translations by an older authority, selected to illustrate different epochs in the development of Buddhism.)

Beal, Samuel: *An Abstract of Four Lectures upon Buddhist Literature in China* (1882). (Further illustrative translations.)

Eitel, Ernest J.: *Handbook of Chinese Buddhism, Being a Buddhist Sanskrit-Chinese Dictionary.* (Useful for brief descriptions of principal Buddhist books. These must be sought, however, by their Sanskrit names.)

Eliot, Sir Charles: *Hinduism and Buddhism*, III, 281–302. (Probably the best systematic account for the general reader.)

Nanjio, Bunyiu: *A Catalogue of the Chinese Translation of the Buddhist Tripitaka* (Oxford, 1883). (A standard reference work of fundamental importance. Gives classification, titles in Chinese and Sanskrit, names of translators, dates of translations, and sometimes brief description, for all the works of the Chinese canon.)

McGovern, William Montgomery: *Introduction to Mahayana Buddhism*, pp. 223–27. (Brief classification of the Chinese canon, according to the arrangement of the Tokyo edition.)

Reichelt, Karl L.: *Truth and Tradition in Chinese Buddhism*, pp. 203–27. (Describes general characteristics of Buddhist literature, with special attention to certain classics in current use.)

Reischauer, August Karl: *Studies in Japanese Buddhism*,

pp. 158–82. (Discusses the Chinese canon, giving also positions of Japanese scholars with regard to it.)

Wieger, Leon: *Buddhisme chinois*, I, 115–32. (Gives an Index of the authors and translators of Chinese Buddhist literature arranged chronologically.)

b) Outline (after Eliot)

1: General classes of works in the Chinese Tripitaka

(*a*) Sutras (called "Ching" in Chinese), 1,081 works: classics

(1) Mahayana sutras, 541 works in seven classes

(2) Hinayana sutras, 240 works

(3) Mahayana and Hinayana sutras, 300 works

(*a*) These were admitted into the canon under the Sung and Yuan dynasties, 960–1368 A.D.

(*b*) Vinaya-pitaka (or Lü-tsang), 85 works: ritual

(1) Mahayana ritualistic books, among them being

(*a*) *Fan-wang-ching:* the standard manual for the monastic life since the eighth century (text and French translation of this in J. J. M. de Groot's *Le code du Mahayana en Chine*, pp. 14–88)

(2) Hinayana ritualistic books

(*a*) "Compromising five substantial recensions of the whole code, besides extracts, compendiums and manuals"

(*c*) Abhidharma-pitaka (or Lun-tsang), 154 works: philosophical treatises

(1) Mahayana works

(*a*) These have no connection with the Pali Abhidharma but are philosophical treatises ascribed to Asvaghosha, Nagarjuna, Asanga, Vasubandhu, and others

(1) They include three works supposed to have been revealed to Asanga by Maitreya

(2) Hinayana works

(*a*) These also do not correspond to the Pali but are based on Abhidharma works of the Sarvastivadin school

(3) Mahayana and Hinayana texts admitted into the canon after A.D. 960

(*d*) Miscellaneous works (or Tsa-tsang), 342 works
- (1) Translations of Indian miscellaneous works
- (2) Works originally composed in Chinese; these include
  - (*a*) Historical works, such as
    - (1) General histories of Buddhism
    - (2) Collections of ecclesiastical biography
    - (3) Travels of various pilgrims who visited India
  - (*b*) Critical works; these include
    - (1) Thirteen catalogues of the Tripitaka at different periods, encyclopedic arrangements of extracts from the Tripitaka, concordances of numerical categories, a dictionary of Sanskrit terms, etc.
  - (*c*) Literature of several Chinese sects
    - (1) Works of the T'ien-T'ai, Hwa Yen, Lü (Vinaya), and Chan (Contemplative) schools
  - (*d*) Controversial literature
    - (1) Polemics against Taoism (collected between 71 and 730 A.D.
    - (2) Replies to attacks by Confucian scholars
    - (3) Refutations of objections raised by skeptics or heretics
  - (*e*) Other miscellaneous works such as prefaces and laudatory verses, memoirs of remarkable monks, etc.

2. There were twelve different collections of the Tripitaka made between the years 518 and 1737 A.D. by order of different emperors (see Nanjio, p. xxvii, and Eliot, III, 289)
   - (*a*) The first seven of these were in manuscript only
   - (*b*) The last five (from 971 A.D. onward) were printed
3. For the chronological table of the thirteen catalogues still

in existence see Nanjio, pp xiii–xxii, and Eliot, III, 290; these date from 520 to 1600 A.D.

(*a*) The successive catalogues reveal a certain amount of shifting, some works being added and some dropped out with the passage of time

4. For the different editions of the Tripitaka see Nanjio, p. xxviii; Eliot, III, 291; and Wieger, pp. 112–14
5. Problems involved in the investigation of the Chinese Tripitaka (Eliot, III, 293–99)
   (*a*) The determination of dates and authorship of translations
      (1) Chinese scholars are usually safe guides here
   (*b*) The uncertainty of faithfulness in translations, for
      (1) A method often followed was for an Indian to explain the text to a literary Chinese who recast the explanation in his own language
      (2) Some translators gave only abstracts
      (3) Some either amplified or transposed their material, or combined different texts into one
      (4) Others made literal, word-for-word renderings which are scarcely intelligible
   (*c*) The text used by the translator was often different from the Pali or Sanskrit text that we possess
6. For general character of some of the more common Buddhist literature see Reichelt, pp. 203–27
   (*a*) Interesting evidence of the veneration in which Buddhists hold their scriptures will be found in *ibid.*, pp. 213–14
   (*b*) Scriptures most commonly used in China
      (1) Hua-yen Ching (Sanskrit: Buddhavatamsaka Sutra), Nanjio, Nos. 87–89
      (2) Leng-yen Ching (Sanskrit: Surangama Sutra), Nanjio, No. 399 (see Beal, *Catena*, pp. 284–369)
      (3) Pure Land scriptures: Wu-liang-shou Ching, Fu-shuo O-mi-t'o Ching, Kuan-Wu-liang-shou Ching (SBE, Vol. XLIX)

(4) Miao-fa Lien-hua Ching (Saddharma Pundarika Sutra), Nanjio, Nos. 134–39 (see *ibid.*, Vol. XXI)
(5) Chin-kang Ching (Vajracchedika Sutra) (see *ibid.*, Vol. XLIX)
(6) Ch'i Hsin Lun (Mahayana sraddhotpada sastra), "The Awakening of Faith" (see above, pp. 26 and 30)

VI. Monastic Life in China

a) References

Beal, Samuel: *Catena of Chinese Scriptures*, pp. 204–44. (Translations of the Chinese *Pratimoksha* and the *Daily Manual of the Shaman* [or priest].)

Boerschmann, Ernst: *Chinesische Architectur* (1925). 2 vols. (A thoroughgoing study of temple and other forms; large plates, plans, drawings, detail, etc.)

Boerschmann, Ernst: *Picturesque China: Architecture and Landscape.* (Includes many fine temple pictures.)

Eliot, Sir Charles: *Hinduism and Buddhism*, III, 321–35. (Good summary of available scholarly information.)

Groot, J. J. M. de: *Le code du Mahayana en Chine.* (Translations of the ritualistic books in which the monks are instructed and full description of the ordination ceremonies.)

Hackmann, H.: *Buddhism as a Religion*, pp. 218–30, 245–48. (A description of essentials, and a criticism of the character of Chinese monasticism.)

Hackmann, H.: "*Pai chang ch'ing kuei:* The Rules of Buddhist Monastic Life in China," *T'oung Pao*, 1908, pp. 651–62. (Summarizes the contents of an eighth-century monastic manual which is still authoritative.)

Johnston, R. F.: *Buddhist China*, pp. 122–69 on "Pilgrimages" and pp. 230–58 on "Monks and Monasteries of Chiu-Hwa."

Melchers, Bernd: *China: Der Tempelbau: Die Lochan von Ling-yän-sï* (Hagen, 1921). (Excellent pictures of temple buildings, both exterior and interior views, with ground plans, elevations, etc.; images of *lohans*.)

Milne, W. C.: *Life in China* (1858), pp. 134–45. (On nuns and nunneries.)

Reichelt, Karl L.: *Truth and Tradition in Chinese Buddhism*, pp. 228–97 on "Monastic Life" and "Pilgrimages"; also pp. 77–126 on "Masses for the Dead." (Written with great insight out of an experience of twenty years of life and work among Buddhist priests.)

Wieger, Leon: *Bouddhisme chinois*, Tome I. (For translations of the literature of ordination and other monastic regulations.)

b) Outline

1. Where monks come from
   - (*a*) Most are given into the monastic life as children by families in straitened circumstances (Hackmann, *Buddhism*, p. 218; Reichelt, pp. 229–30)
     - (1) Each boy is under the tutelage of some monk until time of ordination (cf. Ceylonese practice, pp. 50–51 above)
   - (*b*) Some enter as adults from various causes (Reichelt, pp. 231–33)
     - (1) Sorrow and trouble in the outside world
     - (2) Desire to seek refuge from consequences of crime
     - (3) Genuine desire for religious light, comfort, and peace
     - (4) Sickness (not infrequently healed)
     - (5) Old age and loneliness, including desire to prepare for death
   - (*c*) The social classes from which monks are derived
     - (1) The common people furnish the great majority
     - (2) The upper classes furnish a minority which constitutes material for most of the leadership
   - (*d*) Nuns come chiefly from circumstances of domestic break-up (Reichelt, p. 234; for details on nuns and nunneries see Milne, referred to above)

2. The course of instruction leading to ordination
   (*a*) Training as novices in the routine of daily worship
      (1) Usually a matter of some years, but omitted in the case of those entering as adults (Reichelt, p. 236)
   (*b*) Instruction in the law
      (1) The commandments of the Hinayana
         (*a*) The ten great commandments (Reichelt, pp. 241 and 242; Wieger, I, 153)
         (*b*) The two hundred and fifty commandments of the Pratimoksha (Beal, pp. 204–39; a description of the use of this in the ceremony of penitence, or Uposatha, is in De Groot, pp. 172–95)
      (2) The fifty-eight commandments of the Fan-wang Ching (or *sutra* of Brahma's net; not the same as Brahmajala *sutta* of the Pali canon)
         (*a*) For text and translation see De Groot, pp. 1–88; he gives an analysis of its ideas on pp. 89–98
         (*b*) For a brief description in English see Eliot, III, 322–25
      (3) This training, which lasts from sixty to ninety days, is severe (for detail see Reichelt, pp. 237–39)
3. The ordination ceremony (For a clear description of the essentials of this read *ibid.*, pp. 239–47. For a full scholarly account, including translations from the text used, read De Groot, pp. 207–56. A very brief statement will be found in Hackmann, *Buddhism*, pp. 219–20)
   (*a*) The three stages of ordination (according to De Groot)
      (1) That by which the candidate becomes a *sramanera* (*shami*, in Chinese), or holy one of the lowest degree
         (*a*) The main thing here is the acceptance of the ten primary vows
      (2) That by which the candidate becomes a *sraman* or *bhikshu* (*pi-ch'iu* in Chinese), the *arhat* of the Hinayana

(a) The acceptance of the vows of the Pratimoksha

(3) That by which the candidate becomes a Bodhisattva (*p'u-sa* in Chinese), or full follower of the Mahayana

(a) The acceptance of the vows of the Fan-wang Ching

(b) This terminates with the branding of spots in the scalp, three to eighteen according to the zeal of the candidate

(1) These symmetrically arranged spots betoken ever after the avowed priest

(2) On the significance of this practice see Eliot, III, 328–30

NOTE.—The reader will observe that Reichelt differs from De Groot in putting the vows of the Pratimoksha into the first stage, the vows of the Fan-wang Ching into the second, and giving four special vows for the third stage (p. 245). De Groot's observations were made in Fukien and Reichelt's in Nanking.

4. After ordination a monk is assured of a welcome in any of the monasteries throughout China and even in neighboring Buddhist countries (Reichelt, pp. 247–48)
5. Monastery buildings: for descriptions of these the following may be consulted
   (a) Eliot, III, 325–27
   (b) Hackmann, *Buddhism*, pp. 201–6
   (c) Reichelt, pp. 247–65
   (d) Johnston, esp. chaps. x, xi, xiii
   (e) For pictures consult Boerschmann and Melchers, listed above
6. The organization of a monastery (after Reichelt, pp. 265–71)
   (a) The administrative department
      (1) The abbot (*fan-chang*) is the nominal head

(2) A retired abbot still in the monastery, however, may retain a decisive vote

(3) The abbot is assisted by other senior monks

(a) The head is the *tu-chien*, or manager

(b) With him are the *fu-ssu*, or assistant managers

(c) These manage funds, property, and purchases

(b) The guest department

(1) The head here is the main host (*chih-k'o*)

(a) He is assisted by the *seng chih*, or inspector

(2) These manage everything connected with the entertaining of guests

(c) The department of instruction and worship

(1) The chief here is the instructor (*wei-na*)

(2) He and his assistants arrange the hours of meditation, the masses, the insignia of worship, etc.

(d) Other minor offices connected with the dining-room, smaller chapels and halls, sweeping, cleaning, etc.

(e) The east and west parties

(1) This is a division of the monks during worship and meal times

(a) The west party consists of the members of the administrative and guest departments

(b) The east party consists of members of the department of worship

(2) All important guests stand with the west party, which is the more honorable

7. Activities of the monks

(a) Services of daily worship (Reichelt, pp. 272–76; Hackmann, *Buddhism*, p. 221; Eliot, III, 331)

(b) Attendance at certain special times on religious lectures (Reichelt, pp. 277–78)

(c) Meditation (Hackmann, *Buddhism*, pp. 222–23; De Groot, pp. 169 f.; Reichelt, pp. 278–83)

(d) Performance of rituals connected with festivals and special days (Hackmann, *Buddhism*, pp. 221–22; *T'oung Pao*, 1908, p. 661; Eliot, III, 332) (*e*) Performance of masses for the dead (Reichelt gives a full description and explanation in a highly important chapter, pp. 77–126; a brief treatment is given in Hackman, *Buddhism*, pp. 229 f.; De Groot, pp. 144–47; and Eliot, III, 333–34)

(*f*) Pilgrimages (Johnston, pp. 122–69; Reichelt, pp. 284–97; Hackmann, *Buddhism*, pp. 252–53)

VII. Present-Day Buddhism in China

a) References

Hodous, Lewis: *Buddhism and Buddhists in China*, pp. 19–71. (Buddhism in relation to the peasant, the family, and social life; its conception of the future life and its spiritual values. Recent tendencies to reform.)

Millican, Frank R.: "T'ai Hsü and Modern Buddhism," *Chinese Recorder*, 1923, pp. 326–32. (Describes the work of the Buddhist reformer, T'ai Hsü.)

Millican, Frank R.: "Buddhism in the Light of Modern Thought as Interpreted by the Monk T'ai Hsü," *ibid.*, 1926, pp. 91–94. (Based on T'ai Hsü's book, *The Science of the Philosophy of Life.*)

Pratt, J. B.: *The Pilgrimage of Buddhism*, pp. 352–416. (Excellent observation by a Western philosopher of the Buddhist layman, the Buddhist revival, and Buddhist thought as found in China today.)

Reichelt, Karl L.: *Truth and Tradition in Chinese Buddhism*, pp. 298–311. (Informal observations on certain aspects.)

Tsu, Yu Yue: "Present Tendencies in Chinese Buddhism," *Journal of Religion*, 1921, pp. 497–512. (Describes the various attempts at reform that have arisen in Buddhism since the revolution of 1911, especially that of T'ai Hsü.)

Tsu, Yu Yue: "Diary of a Chinese Buddhist Nun, T'ze Kuang," *ibid.*, 1927, pp. 612–18. (Translated from the Buddhist periodical, *Hai Ch'ao Yin.* A case of contemporary Buddhist religious experience.)

b) Outline

1. The last twenty-five years
   (*a*) Since 1902, partly under the influence of Japanese leadership, Chinese Buddhism has participated in the growing tendency of Buddhism everywhere to become conscious of itself, its past history, and its mission to the world (Hodous, pp. 63–64, 70–71)
2. Events leading up to the revolution of 1911 were immediately responsible for the earliest reforming movements (Tsu, "Present Tendencies, etc.," *op. cit.*, pp. 498–99)
   (*a*) Earliest activities
      (1) The formation of a number of Buddhist societies, the most important of which was the Chinese National Buddhist Society (Chung Hua Fu Chiao Tsung Hui) in 1910
         (*a*) The aim was to purify the monastic order of the ignorance and mercenary spirit of the monks (*ibid.*, p. 500)
         (*b*) It found an added function in the struggle for religious liberty in the early days of the republic (Reichelt, pp. 304–5)
         (*c*) Magazines were published and fellowship promoted
      (2) This first movement, however, failed for
         (*a*) It was political rather than religious in character
         (*b*) It encountered hostility from the government
            (1) In 1915 was promulgated the "Regulations for Government Supervision of Temples and Monasteries" (Tsu, "Present Tendencies, etc.," *op. cit.*, p. 502; Reichelt, p. 305)
            (2) When the Buddhists protested through their National Society the government closed the organization
      (3) General activities, indicative of revival, continued

(a) These, on to the present, have been
(1) Rehabilitation of monasteries and temples, increase of accessions to the religion, increase of publications, use of popular lectures, formation of Buddhist societies, and attempts to socialize Buddhism (Hodous, pp. 65–68)

3. The religious revival began in 1915 under the leadership of the monk T'ai Hsü
(a) T'ai Hsü had the spiritual qualifications for such leadership
(1) For a brief statement of the facts of his early life see Millican, "T'ai Hsü, etc.," *op. cit.*, p. 327
(2) For an autobiographical sketch revealing the spirit of the man see Tsu, "Present Tendencies, etc.," *op. cit.*, pp. 505 ff.
(b) In his work T'ai Hsü has had the co-operation of many earnest lay devotees (Reichelt, p. 301)
(c) Weaknesses of Buddhism as seen by T'ai Hsü
(1) Lack of efficient organization for the propagation of the religion
(2) Corruption of the monastic order
(d) His plans for reform (*Jour. of Relig.*, 1921, p. 507, and *Chinese Recorder*, 1923, p. 328)
(1) A national system of Buddhist institutions, religious, charitable, and educational
(2) A national monastery and university at the capital of the country with library and a museum for Buddhist art
(a) He would put all images of this institution into the museum, for while he tolerates idolatry for the masses he rejects it in his higher teaching
(3) Stricter discipline as well as manual labor for the monks
(4) Propaganda work by means of
(a) Publications, including the periodical *Hai*

Ch'ao Yin ("Sound of the Tide"), which is the organ of the reform

(*b*) The formation of Buddhist societies

(*c*) Public lectures

(*d*) The conduct of orphanages and the visitation of jails

(*e*) Actually much of T'ai Hsü's activity has been carried on at the Wuchang Buddhist Academy and the Buddhist Lecture Hall in Kuling (*Chinese Recorder*, 1923, p. 329, and Reichelt, pp. 301–3)

(*f*) The movement has had its effect in stimulating certain kinds of religious experiences (for which see the latter part of Tsu's article, *op. cit.*, 1921, and all of the article in the same periodical for 1927)

(*g*) For its intellectual influence see the regulations of the Hangchow Buddhist Philosophical Club, *Chinese Recorder*, 1923, p. 329

(*h*) For an example of T'ai Hsü's teaching read Millican, *ibid.*, 1926, pp. 91–94

(*i*) The great problem (*Jour. Relig.*, 1921, pp. 511–12)

(1) How can Buddhism adjust itself to modern conditions without becoming something essentially different?

4. The intellectual revival

(*a*) This is promoted at a Buddhist academy at Nanking under the leadership of an old Confucian scholar by the name of Ou-yang Ching-wu (Reichelt, p. 303)

(1) The aim here is a critical study of texts and the understanding of Mahayanist philosophy

(2) Noted contemporary scholars, among them Liang Ch'i-ch'ao and Liang Shu-ming, have studied Buddhism with Ou-yang

(*b*) The activities of this school result in revised texts, compilations, translations, etc., and the stimulation of book study

5. The tendency to revive the Mi-Tsung (or "School of Mystery")
   (*a*) This school, which is of the Tantric variety, appeared in China in the eighth century but later died out or became simply an aspect of other schools (Eliot, III, 316–18)
   (*b*) It became the Shingon sect in Japan from where it is now being relearned (Reichelt, pp. 309–10)
   (*c*) In 1926 Mongolian Lamaist representatives of this school were invited to perform their services in many chief cities of Northern and Central China

PART IV

IN JAPAN: THE TOPMOST TURN

I. The Introduction of Buddhism into Japan and the Rise of the Early Sects

a) References

Anesaki, Masaharu: *Buddhist Art in Its Relation to Buddhist Ideals* (1915).

Armstrong, Robert Cornell: *Buddhism and Buddhists in Japan* (1927), pp. 4–14 and 50–67. (Excellent introduction to Japanese Buddhism; annotated Bibliography.)

Coates, H. H., and Ishizuka, R.: *Honen the Buddhist Saint* (1925), pp. 1–27. (Special attention to the adjustment of Shinto to the new religion from the Continent.)

Griffis, W. E.: *The Religions of Japan* (1895).

Hackmann, H.: *Buddhism as a Religion*, pp. 88–92 (on the introduction) and 286–92 (on the sects).

Harada, Tasuku: *The Faith of Japan*, pp. 13–20. (Clear and brief.)

Knox, G. W.: *Development of Religion in Japan*, Lecture III, pp. 80–113. (Broad interpretative treatment.)

Lloyd, Arthur: "Developments of Japanese Buddhism," *Transactions of the Asiatic Society of Japan*, XXII (1894), 361–405. (A more technical account of the sects.)

Lloyd, Arthur: *The Creed of Half Japan* (1911), pp. 168–258. (Concrete historical account.)

Nanjio, Bunyiu: *A Short History of the Twelve Japanese Buddhist Sects*, pp. 1–103. (A valuable summary by a noted Japanese scholar of the last generation.)

Okuma, S.: *Fifty Years of New Japan* (1909), pp. 65–75. (Good summary of Japanese Buddhism by J. Takakusu.)

Reischauer, August K.: *Studies in Japanese Buddhism*, pp. 79–102. (A clear exposition of the essentials.)

Saunders, Kenneth J.: *Epochs of Buddhist History* (1924), pp. 163–72. (A suggestive description.)

b) Outline

1. Introduction of Buddhism into Japan
   (*a*) Buddhism entered Japan by way of Korea, but the exact date of its first entry is unknown
      (1) For Japan's earliest relations with Korea see Lloyd, *Creed*, pp. 168–72
   (*b*) The traditional formal entry was in the sixth century A.D.
      (1) In 552 A.D. the ruler of the Korean state of Kudara, in homage of the Japanese emperor, sent to the latter
         (*a*) An image of Buddha
         (*b*) Scriptures and works of art
         (*c*) A message designed to recommend Buddhism to Japan
      (2) The outbreak of a pestilence shortly after the acceptance of these precipitated a struggle between antagonistic court parties over the new religion (Reischauer, pp. 81 f., and Lloyd, *Creed*, pp. 173 f.)
         (*a*) Conservatives opposed Buddhism in the name of loyalty to the national Shinto gods
         (*b*) Liberals contended for it as the exponent of the higher civilization of the Continent
      (3) Buddhism came gradually to prevail because the higher quality of its culture appealed to the emperors and rulers
         (*a*) The Empress Suiko (593–628 A.D.) became a devoted Buddhist
         (*b*) During her reign the crown prince, Shotoku Taishi, in actual control of the government, sought in every way to promote the new religion (Lloyd, *Creed*, pp. 178–90)
            (1) A constitution was established with Buddhism as its foundation (Armstrong, p. 6)

(2) Monasteries and philanthropic institutions were set up (Okuma, p. 66)

(3) Missionaries came from Korea and China, while Japanese Buddhists traveled to the Continent for study (Reischauer, p. 84)

(4) Art was stimulated as an instrument for the promotion of religious ideals (see Anesaki, *Buddhist Art*, pp. 20–22)

2. Rise of the early sects

(*a*) Sects of the Nara period (710–94)

(1) Sanron sect (the "Three-śastra" sect)

(*a*) Introduced from Korea in 625 A.D. by Ekwan

(*b*) Teaches the Madhyamaka doctrine of Nagarjuna (see above, pp. 27 f.)

(*c*) Its middle path is the doctrine that "the truth is nothing but the state where thoughts come to an end" (Armstrong, p. 54)

(2) Jojitsu sect (Satya-siddhi-sastra sect)

(*a*) Introduced about the same time as the Sanron

(*b*) Teaches the emptiness of self and all things (see Armstrong, pp. 52–53)

(3) Hosso sect (Dharma-lakshana sect)

(*a*) Brought from China about the middle of the seventh century by Dosho (Reischauer, p. 86)

(*b*) Teaches the Yoga or Vijnana doctrine (see above, pp. 28–30)

(*c*) The character of the doctrine of this school made possible a special adjustment to Shinto (see Lloyd, *Creed*, pp. 200–201)

(4) Kusha sect (Abhidharma-kosa-sastra sect)

(*a*) Introduced in 658 A.D. by two Japanese priests who had studied in China (Reischauer, p. 86)

(*b*) The best representative of orthodox southern Buddhism (Armstrong, p. 53)

(5) Kegon sect (Avataṁsaka-sutra sect)

(*a*) Brought to Japan in 736 A.D.

(*b*) The first sect of the true Mahayana school in Japan (Reischauer, p. 86)
(*c*) Its chief scripture, the Avatamsaka Sutra, was supposed to have been preached by Sakyamuni immediately after attaining enlightenment (Lloyd, *Creed*, p. 203)
(*d*) Its main doctrine is that of the Absolute Law Body (or Buddha essence), immanent in all things (for description and significance see Armstrong, pp. 57–60)
(6) Ritsu sect (Vinaya or ritualistic sect)
(*a*) Introduced into Japan as a separate organization in 754 A.D., though the Vinaya teachings were among the earliest known to the Japanese
(*b*) It was essentially the Hinayana system of discipline as revised by Dharmagupta (for detail see Lloyd, *Creed*, pp. 131–44)
(*c*) It was eventually absorbed into the Mahayana sects (Reischauer, p. 87; Lloyd, *Creed*, p. 165)
(*b*) These sects are to be regarded as schools of thought within the priesthood rather than as separate institutions
(*c*) For the place of Buddhism in the culture of the Nara epoch see Reischauer, pp. 87–89
(*d*) On the sculpture and architecture of the period see Anesaki, pp. 22–26, and accompanying plates
(*e*) Eventually the meddling of the priests in politics caused the emperor to remove his capital to Kyoto (Lloyd, *Creed*, pp. 226–28)
(*f*) The Kyoto sects, ninth century A.D.
(1) Tendai sect
(*a*) Founded by Dengyō Daishi (Saichō)
(1) A good account of his life is given in Lloyd, *Creed*, pp. 225–36
(*b*) Following the T'ien-T'ai sect of China (see above, pp. 60 f.), it bases itself on the Saddharma

Pundarika Sutra (Lloyd gives a brief analysis of this in *Transactions of the Asiatic Society of Japan*, XXII, 374–78)

- (1) For a good statement of the inclusive quality of this teaching see Armstrong, pp. 60–66

(*c*) But to the original T'ien-T'ai the Japanese Tendai added elements derived from other sects, thus making the whole an eclecticism (see Reischauer, pp. 92–94, and *ASJ*, XXII, 381–82)

(*d*) For an account of the unifying character of Tendai as well as of its weakness see Saunders, pp. 168–72

(2) Shingon sect

(*a*) Founded by Kōbō Daishi (774–835 A.D.)

- (1) For a brief account of his life see Reischauer, pp. 94–95
- (2) For a more extended account see Lloyd in the *Trans. Asiat. Soc. Japan*, XXII, 382–87, and in the *Creed of Half Japan*, pp. 233–36 and 243–58

(*b*) The teachings of Shingon give the Japanese form of the school of Mantra Buddhism

- (1) The emphasis is upon mystical absorption in the Infinite, conceived as the center of a metaphysical world of ideas behind the phenomenal world (Knox, p. 99; Armstrong, pp. 65–67)
- (2) For a full exposition see Lloyd, *Trans. Asiat. Soc. Japan*, pp. 382–405
- (3) Much use is made of magic and mystery (see Reischauer, p. 97)
  - (*a*) Shingon priests are skilful users of ritual hand-poses (*mudras*), which are symbols of mystic meanings (for pic-

tures of this sort of thing see Tyra de Kleen's *Mudras*, which though copied from the priests of Bali in Java are yet typical)

(*b*) For the influence and use of secret symbolism in art see Anesaki, pp. 31–46

(4) Religious healing is practiced (see Saunders, pp. 190–91)

(5) By its teaching that all spiritual beings are emanations of the eternal Buddha, Vairochana, the Shingon sect led in the absorption of the Shinto pantheon by Buddhism (see Reischauer, pp. 98–99; an extended account of this syncretism will be found in Griffis, *Religions of Japan*, pp. 191–223)

(3) The wealth and success of the Buddhism of the ninth century were accompanied by moral and spiritual decline (Reischauer, 100–102; Lloyd, *Creed*, pp. 141–42)

II. Sects of the Great Awakening

a) References

Anesaki, Masaharu: *Nichiren the Buddhist Prophet* (1916). (An effective portrayal of the founder of one of the great sects.)

Armstrong, R. C.: *Buddhism and Buddhists in Japan*, pp. 79–96.

Coates, H. H., and Ishizuka, R.: *Honen the Buddhist Saint* (1925). (A translation of the authorized life of the founder of the Jodo sect, with historical Introduction and notes, explanatory and critical. A mine of information on Pure Land Buddhism.)

Griffis, W. E.: *Religions of Japan* (1895), pp. 251–86.

Haas, Hans: *Amida Buddha: Unsere Zuflucht* (1910). (Translations of important sources for the Jodo sect. Valuable for detailed study.)

Knox, George W.: *Development of Religion in Japan* (1907), pp. 114–37. (Good general sketch of the Pure Land and Nichiren teachings.)

Lloyd, Arthur: "Developments of Japanese Buddhism," *Transactions of the Asiatic Society of Japan*, XXII (1894), 405–49.

Lloyd, Arthur: *Shinran and His Work* (1910). (Deals fully with the Shin sect and its teachings. Chap. iii treats of the life of Shinran.)

Lloyd, Arthur: *Creed of Half Japan* (1911), pp. 259–328.

Nanjio, Bunyiu: *A Short History of Twelve Japanese Buddhist Sects* (1886), pp. 104–47. (A valuable summary by a noted Japanese scholar of the last generation.)

Nukariya, Kaiten: *The Religion of the Samurai, a Study of Zen Philosophy and Discipline in China and Japan* (1913).

Reischauer, A. K.: *Studies in Japanese Buddhism* (1917), pp. 102–31.

Satomi, Kishio: *Japanese Civilization* (1924).

Saunders, K. J.: *Epochs in Buddhist History* (1924), pp. 172–85.

For expositions of the teachings of the great sects by modern Japanese Buddhists the reader should consult the many useful articles in the *Eastern Buddhist* (published bimonthly, Kyoto, May, 1921——) and the *Young East* (monthly, Tokyo, June, 1925——).

b) Outline

1. Religious need, reacting to the worldly corruption of the Buddhism of the ninth century, brought about the rise of great reforming sects in the twelfth and thirteenth centuries (Reischauer, p. 102)
2. Jōdo sect (first of the Japanese Pure Land sects; cf. above, pp. 61–63)
   (*a*) Pure Land practice before the founding of Jōdo
      (1) The "Dancing Nembutsu" of the priest Kuya (903–72)
         (*a*) This was an attempt to arouse the people reli-

giously by going about the country dancing and repeating the prayer to Amitabha (in Japanese, Namu-Amida-Butsu)

(*b*) See Lloyd, *Creed*, pp. 242 and 264–68; Coates and Ishizuka, p. 36

(2) The Tendai "Nembutsu" (Coates and Ishizuka, pp. 37–38)

(*a*) "Invocation of Amitabha" (Nembutsu) for the cultivation of meditative ecstasy

(*b*) Promoted especially by Genshin (942–1017)

(1) See Reischauer, pp. 102–4

(3) The "Yūdzū Nembutsu" of Ryōnin Shonin (1072–1132)

(*a*) A society for "mutual benefit through Nembutsu" (see Coates and Ishizuka, p. 39, and Reischauer, pp. 104–5)

(*b*) Hōnen and the foundation of the Jōdo sect

(1) Conditions against which Hōnen reacted

(*a*) Political confusion due to rivalry of ruling clans

(*b*) General illiteracy and moral degeneracy

(*c*) Ritualism and magic in religion for the sake of material goods

(*d*) Luxury and worldliness of the clergy

(*e*) Unspiritual doctrinal conceptions

(2) The life of Hōnen (1133–1212)

(*a*) Read Coates and Ishizuka for the full translation of the Japanese authorized biography

(*b*) Brief sketches will be found in Reischauer, pp. 106–8, and Lloyd, *Creed*, pp. 272–73

(3) For translations (in German) of certain of Hōnen's writings and letters see Haas

(4) Hōnen's distinctive contribution (Coates and Ishizuka, p. 42)

(*a*) He rejected meditation and complete comprehension as unnecessary

(b) He insisted on simple faith as the one essential accompaniment to the invocation of Buddha's name (see also Armstrong, p. 84, and Reischauer, p. 107)

(c) The Jōdo system, a religion of despair rather than of hope

(1) It is salvation not through ethical conformity to an ideal but through blind trust in the merits of Amitabha and the ceaseless repetition of pious formulas (Lloyd, *Trans. Asiat. Soc. Japan*, XXII, 411–22)

3. Shin sect (or true sect of the Pure Land)

(a) Founded by Hōnen's greatest disciple, Shinran Shōnin

(1) For the life of Shinran see Lloyd, *Shinran*, pp. 15–32; Armstrong, pp. 87–89; Reischauer, pp. 108–10

(2) Shinran (1173–1262) carried the doctrine of salvation by faith to its logical conclusion

(a) Faith in Amitabha is the essential. Good works and even repetition of Buddha's name are mere accompaniments (Coates and Ishizuka, pp. 51–52)

(b) By marrying Shinran demonstrated that celibacy is unnecessary to salvation and that even the dweller in the midst of ordinary life may be saved by faith (Griffis, pp. 271–72)

(c) For the practical consequences see Armstrong, pp. 89–91

(3) The teachings of the Shin sect represent a development of Buddhism that contrasts with the original religion of Gotama (Knox, pp. 129–35; Reischauer, pp. 110–15)

(a) Salvation in the Western Paradise instead of Nirvana

(b) Participation in all human relationships instead of flight from the world

(c) Salvation through faith in another instead of one's own efforts

(*d*) Worship of a god, Amitabha (Amida in Japanese), instead of indifference to such beings
(*e*) Continuity and identity of the individual into a future life instead of denial of such continuity and identity

(4) For detailed exposition of the teachings see Lloyd, Shinran, pp. 27–153, and in *Trans. Asiat. Soc. Japan*, pp. 413–30; also Haas, pp. 28–37 and 116–66
(5) A brief but vivid picture of the Shin sect will be found in Saunders, pp. 176–80

4. Zen sect: the Japanese "Meditative" (Dhyāna) school; cf. above, pp. 59 f.
   (*a*) Zen (or Dhyāna) teachings were introduced into Japan as early as the seventh century (Nukariya, *The Religion of the Samurai*, p. 28)
   (*b*) As a sect Zen was established in three branches
      (1) Rinzai, founded by Eisai in 1191 (*ibid.*, pp. 28–30)
      (2) Sō-Tō, founded by Dō-gen in 1236 (*ibid.*, pp. 30–34)
      (3) O Baku, founded by Yin Yuen in 1654 (*ibid.*, pp. 48–49)
   (*c*) Characteristics of Zen
      (1) The use of paradoxical methods to arouse men from religious indifference (Armstrong, p. 81; Saunders, pp. 142–45)
      (2) The use of scriptures not as authority but as a convenience in the cultivation of intuitive enlightenment (Nukariya, pp. 52–74)
      (3) The practice of sitting in meditation (Zazen) (Reischauer, pp. 118–22; Armstrong, pp. 81–83; Nukariya, pp. 188–97)
      (4) Emphasis upon an experience of immediate, intuitive insight (see Suzuki, "The Revelation of a New Truth in Zen Buddhism," *Eastern Buddhist*, I, 194–228)
   (*d*) For a present-day exposition of Zen teachings by a Jap-

anese Buddhist see articles by Daisetz Teitaro Suzuki in the *Eastern Buddhist* and in his *Essays in Zen Buddhism* (Luzac & Co., 1927)

5. Nichiren sect
   (*a*) The only Japanese sect founded upon a personality rather than upon a doctrine (see Reischauer, p. 126)
   (*b*) For life and times of Nichiren (1222–82) see
      (1) Anesaki, pp. 1–75 (a brilliantly written appreciation)
      (2) Lloyd, *Creed*, pp. 287–98
      (3) Satomi, *Japanese Civilization* (1923), pp. 117–87
   (*c*) Characteristics of Nichirenism
      (1) Interpretation of national ills as the result of defection from true Buddhism (Lloyd, *Creed*, p. 310)
      (2) Attack upon other sects as distorters of the truth (Anesaki, pp. 36–37; Lloyd, *Creed*, pp. 293–95 and 313–24; Reischauer, pp. 123–25; Satomi, pp. 55–65)
      (3) Acceptance of the "Lotus Scripture" (Saddharma-pundarika Sutra), as interpreted by Nichiren, as the basic scripture of Buddhism (an illuminating analysis of this scripture in relation to Nichiren's understanding of it is given by Anesaki, pp. 16–32; see also Satomi, pp. 29–55)
      (4) Exaltation of Sakyamuni in his eternal aspect as the Supreme Being (Lloyd, *Creed*, pp. 298–99; Satomi, pp. 77–94; Anesaki, pp. 76–87)
   (*d*) Nichiren's pugnacious loyalty to his country's welfare makes a strong nationalistic appeal to modern Japanese youth (Armstrong, p. 94; Satomi, pp. 228–31 and 155–57; also the instructive charts in Appendixes IV–VI of Saunders)

III. From the Fourteenth to the Nineteenth Century

a) References

Brinkley, Captain F.: *A History of the Japanese People* (1915), pp. 485–86, 505–6, 577–78, 583.

Griffis, W. E.: *The Mikado's Empire* (1890), pp. 229–35.
Hara, Katsuro: *Introduction to the History of Japan* (1920), pp. 273–81, 351–54. (A Japanese perspective.)
Lloyd, Arthur: *Creed of Half Japan* (1911), pp. 341–80.
Murdoch, James, and Yamagata, Isoh: *A History of Japan during the Century of Early Foreign Intercourse* (1542–1651) (1903), pp. 144–67, 200–202. (Detailed account of certain phases.)
Reischauer, A. K.: *Studies in Japanese Buddhism* (1917), pp. 131–54.

b) Outline

1. During this period there was no new development within Buddhism itself
2. From 1333 to 1550 temples became armed fortresses and monks entered into the political strife of the times while religious spirit declined
3. In the Tokugawa period (1550–1868) the power and influence of Buddhism waned
   (*a*) Its political power was crushed by Nobunaga Hideyoshi
      (1) Nobunaga wiped out the Tendai Monastery in 1571 (Lloyd, p. 358; Murdoch and Yamagata, pp. 164–65)
      (2) In 1580 he subdued the powerful fortress of the Monto branch of the Jōdo sect
      (3) In 1584 Hideyoshi destroyed the Shingon temple-fortress of Negoro (Murdoch and Yamagata, pp. 200–202)
   (*b*) Its wealth was drained by heavy imposts (Lloyd, p. 362)
   (*c*) Under Ieyasu, Buddhism was made subservient to the interests of the rulers
   (*d*) Rival spiritual forces appeared
      (1) Catholic missions from Europe (Brinkley, pp. 530–55)
      (2) Neo-Confucianism (teachings of Chu Hsi and Wang Yang-ming) from China (Reischauer, pp. 143–49)

(3) Neo-Shintoism (*ibid.*, pp. 149–52; Brinkley, 644–50)

4. In the Meiji era (1868–1912)

(*a*) Buddhism was finally disestablished as the state religion (Reischauer, pp. 152–54)

IV. Present-Day Buddhism in Japan

a) References

Anesaki, Masaharu; *Quelques pages de l'histoire religieuse du Japan* (1921), pp. 143–72. (Interesting as showing one phase of the movement of modern religious thought in Japan where Buddhist ideas played a rôle.)

Armstrong, R. C.: *Buddhism and Buddhists in Japan*, pp. 15–49, 68–78.

Armstrong, R. C.: "Popular Buddhism in Japan," *Christian Movement in Japan, Korea and Formosa*, 1922, pp. 91–103.

Chamberlain, B. H., and Mason, W. B.: *A Handbook for Travelers in Japan* (9th ed.), pp. 39–56. (Convenient condensed account of the temples, gods, and goddesses of Japanese Buddhism.)

Erskine, W. H.: *Japanese Customs* (1925). (See chap. vii for a description of a modern Japanese funeral.)

Getty, Alice: *The Gods of Northern Buddhism* (1914). (Useful for the study and identification of images.)

Hackmann, H.: *Buddhism as a Religion*, pp. 269–95.

Noss, C.: "The Religious and Social Activities of Modern Japanese Buddhists," *Christian Movement in Japan, Korea and Formosa*, 1925, pp. 253–85. (Good account of new Buddhist adjustments to modern conditions.)

Pratt, J. B.: *The Pilgrimage of Buddhism*, pp. 495–671. (Comprehensive description of the present state of Japanese Buddhism as observed by an American philosopher seeking a "synthetic view of Buddhism" as a whole. Especially valuable insight into the intellectual phases.)

Reischauer, A. K.: *Studies in Japanese Buddhism*, pp. 307–27.

Reischauer, A. K.: *The Task in Japan* (1926), pp. 101–36. (A popular presentation from a missionary point of view which throws into relief certain aspects of present-day Buddhism.)

Seiren (Blue Lotus): "In Buddhist Temples." Four articles in the *Eastern Buddhist*, Vol. II. (The temples as seen through the eyes and sentiments of a modern Buddhist.)

Visser, M. W. de: *The Arhats in China and Japan* (1923), pp. 182–96. (Full description of a particular ceremony performed in honor of the sixteen *arhats*.)

1. Monastic life in its external features is similar to that of China
   (*a*) Temples (for a systematic description see *Handbook of the Old Shrines and Temples and Their Treasures in Japan*, published in Japan by the Bureau of Religions, Department of Education, containing pictures, plans, descriptions, etc. For verbal descriptions see Hackmann, pp. 271–77, 282–84; Pratt, pp. 503–18; also Seiren as above)
   (*b*) Divinities (see Getty and De Visser, listed above; for brief accounts see Hackmann, pp. 277–82; Pratt, pp. 495–502; and Chamberlain and Mason, pp. 39–56)
   (*c*) Activities of the monks (Hackmann, pp. 284–86; Armstrong, *Christian Movement*, pp. 95–110)
      (1) Ritual observances in the temples
      (2) Recitation of sacred texts
      (3) Meditation (Pratt, p. 528)
      (4) Conduct of funerals (Erskine, chap. vii)
2. In making adjustments to modern conditions Buddhism has in recent times tended to develop social ideals and undertaken various forms of social and philanthropic activity (see Noss, listed above; Armstrong, *Buddhism*, pp. 15–49; and Pratt, pp. 529–31 and 567–95)
3. Relation of Buddhism to the people (Armstrong, *Buddhism*, pp. 15–49)

(a) Its temples and ceremonials are interwoven with the common life
(b) It ministers at funerals, festivals for spirits, and other services for the dead
(c) It places a certain emphasis on moral betterment
(1) Through the spring and autumn festivals
(2) In baptismal and dedication ceremonies

4. Modern Buddhist thought in Japan (Pratt, pp. 596–671)
(a) General characteristics
(1) Liberality
(2) Belief in degrees of truth and reality
(3) An idealistic interpretation of the external world
(4) The Anatta doctrine
(b) Philosophical positions of the different sects
(1) These reveal varying interpretations of traditional doctrines
(2) The concepts suggest to the Western mind conflicts and difficulties similar to those in Western idealism
(3) But in every sect there is a mystic trend which makes central the notion of a Buddha nature in all things, the realization of which is merely adumbrated and suggested by all the varying conceptions of the schools
(c) Philosophical Buddhism and modern science

> The Japanese are indeed much interested in the science of the West; but they are also beginning to realize that the philosophy at the basis of all the branches of the Mahayana is of a sort that it is quite capable of making room for everything that science has yet discovered or is likely to discover. —PRATT, p. 698.

5. For a statement of the problems confronting Buddhism in its modern environment see Reischauer, *Studies*, pp. 314–27; also his more popular statement in *The Task in Japan*, pp. 101–36
6. A modern revival of interest in Shinran and his teachings is noticeable (see articles by Gessho Sasaki, Kogetsu Mino,

and others in the *Eastern Buddhist*, especially Mino's "Shinran Revival of the Last Year," *ibid.*, 1922, pp. 285–91)

(*a*) Modern appreciation of Shinranism springs apparently from the fact that it is the one form of Buddhism that is non-celibate and which stresses the practice of Buddhism within the relations of secular life

7. Japanese Buddhism and Christianity

(*a*) For the most recent viewpoint of Christian missions see the report in *The Jerusalem Meeting of the International Missionary Council*, I, 177–90 and 323–26

(*b*) For the view of a detached observer see Pratt, pp. 723–50

(*c*) For a penetrating Japanese discussion see Anesaki, *Religious and Social Problems of the Orient*, pp. 17–33 and 52–73

BIBLIOGRAPHY[1]

ANESAKI, MASAHARU. *Buddhist Art in Its Relation to Buddhist Ideals.* Boston and New York: Houghton Mifflin, 1915.

———. *Nichiren the Buddhist Prophet.* Cambridge: Harvard University Press, 1916.

———. *Quelques pages de l'histoire religieuse du Japan.* Paris: Bernard, 1921.

———. *The Religious and Social Problems of the Orient.* New York: Macmillan, 1923.

ARMSTRONG, ROBERT CORNELL. *Buddhism and Buddhists in Japan.* New York, 1927.

ARNOLD, SIR EDWIN. *The Light of Asia, or the Great Renunciation.* London, 1890.

BAGCHI, PRABODH CHANDRA. *Le canon bouddhique en Chine: Les traducteurs et les traductions.* "Librairie Orientaliste." Paris: Paul Geuthner, 1926.

BARTH, AUGUSTE. *The Religions of India.* London: Paul, Trench, Trübner, 4th ed., 1906; reissue, 1914.

BEAL, SAMUEL. *Catena of Buddhist Scriptures, from the Chinese.* London, 1871.

———. *The Romantic Legend of Sakya Buddha, from the Chinese-Sanscrit.* London, 1875.

———. *Abstract of Four Lectures on Buddhist Literature in China.* London, 1882.

———. *Buddhism in China.* London: Society for Promoting Christian Knowledge, 1884.

———. *The Life of Hiuen-Tsiang by the Shaman Hwui-li.* London: Paul, Trench, Trübner, 1911.

BIGANDET, PIERRE. *The Life or Legend of Gaudama, the Buddha of the Burmese.* London: Paul, Trench, Trübner, 1911–12.

BINYON, LAURENCE. *Painting in the Far East.*

BOERSCHMANN, ERNST. *Picturesque China: Architecture and Landscape.*

———. *Chinesisch Architectur.* 2 vols. 1925.

BOSE, PHANINDRA NATH. *The Indian Teachers in China.* Madras: Ganesan, 1923.

[1] In a very few instances titles that were not utilized in the text have been included for general reference.

Brewster, Earl H. *The Life of Gotama the Buddha* (compiled exclusively from the Pali canon). London: Paul, Trench, Trübner; New York: Dutton, 1926.

Brinkley, Captain. *A History of the Japanese People.* New York: Encyclopaedia Britannica Co., 1915.

Buddhaghosa. *The Expositor: A Translation of Atthasalini, the Commentary on the Dhamma-Sangani.* By Maung Tin. "Pali Text Society Series," 2 vols. 1920–21.

———. *Visuddhi-Magga, or the Path of Purity.* Part I. Translated in the "Pali Text Society Series." 1922.

Cambridge History of India, Vol. I.

Carus, Paul. *The Gospel of Buddha according to Old Records, Told by Paul Carus* (5th ed.). Chicago: Open Court, 1897.

Cave, Henry W. *The Book of Ceylon.*

Cave, Sydney. *Living Religions of the East.*

Christian Movement in Japan, Korea, and Formosa: A Year Book. Published annually by the Federation of Christian Missions (Japan).

Coates, Harper Havelock, and Ishizuka, Ryugaku. *Honen the Buddhist Saint: His Life and Teaching.* Kyoto: Chionin, 1925.

Coomaraswamy, Ananda Kentish. *Buddha and the Gospel of Buddhism.* New York: Putnam's, 1916.

Copleston, Reginald Stephen. *Buddhism Primitive and Present in Magadha and in Ceylon.* London, New York, Bombay, and Calcutta: Longmans Green, 1908.

Dasgupta, Surendranath. *A History of Indian Philosophy*, Vol. I. Cambridge University Press, 1922.

———. *Hindu Mysticism.* Chicago: Open Court, 1927.

Davids, Mrs. Caroline Augusta (Foley) Rhys. *Buddhism: A Study of the Buddhist Norm.* New York: Holt, 1912.

———. *Buddhist Psychology: An Inquiry into the Analysis and Theory of Mind in Pali Literature.* London: Bell, 1914.

Davids, T. W. Rhys. *Lectures on the Origin and Growth of Religion as Illustrated by Some Points in the History of Indian Buddhism.* New York: Putnam's, 1882.

———. *Buddhism: Its History and Literature.* New York: Putnam's, 1896.

———. *Buddhist India.* New York: Putnam's, 1903.

———. *Buddhism: Being a Sketch of the Life and Teachings of Gautama, the Buddha.* Reprint of rev. ed. London: Society for Promoting Christian Knowledge, 1912.

DORE, HENRI. *Researches into Chinese Superstitions.* 7 vols. China: Tusewei, 1914–20.

EDKINS, REV. JOSEPH. *Chinese Buddhism.* Trübner's "Oriental Series." London, 1893.

EITEL, ERNEST JOHN. *Handbook of Chinese Buddhism.* Hongkong: Lane Crawford, 1888.

ELIOT, SIR CHARLES EDGECUMBE. *Hinduism and Buddhism.* 3 vols. London: Arnold, 1921.

ERSKINE, W. H. *Japanese Customs*, 1925.

FARQUHAR, J. N. *An Outline of the Religious Literature of India.* Oxford University Press, 1920.

FENOLLOSA, E. F. *Epochs of Chinese and Japanese Art.* London: W. Heinemann, 1921. 2 vols.

FOCILLON, HENRI. *L'art bouddhique.* Paris: Henri Laurens, 1921.

FOUCHER, ALFRED. *Etude sur l'iconographie bouddhique de l'Inde, d'après des documents nouveaux.* Paris: A. Leroux, 1900–1905.

———. *L'art greco-bouddhique du Gandhara: Etude sur les origines de l'influence classique dans l'art bouddhique de l'Inde et de l'Extrême-Orient.* 3 vols. Paris: Leroux, 1905.

———. "The Beginnings of Buddhist Art" and other essays in *Indian and Central-Asian Archaeology.* Paris: Geuthner, 1917.

GEMMEL, WILLIAM. *The Diamond Sutra (Ching-Kang-Chin) or Prajna-Paramita.* Translated from the Chinese with Introduction and notes. London, 1912.

GETTY, ALICE. *Gods of Northern Buddhism.* Oxford: Clarendon Press, 1914.

GILES, H. A. *The Travels of Fa-hsien (399–414 A.D.), or Record of the Buddhistic Kingdoms.* Cambridge, 1923.

GOGERLY, D. J. *Ceylon Buddhism*, Ed. Arthur Stanley Bishop. 2 vols. London: Paul, Trench, Trübner, 1908.

GRAY, JAMES. *Buddhaghosuppatti, or the Historical Romance of the Rise and Career of Buddhaghosa.* London: Luzac, 1892.

GRIFFIS, W. E. *The Religions of Japan.* New York: Scribner's, 1907.

———. *The Mikado's Empire.* New York: Harper, 1890.

GRIFFITHS, JOHN. *The Paintings in the Buddhist Cave-Temples of Ajanta, Khandesh, India.* 2 vols. London, 1896–97.

GROOT, J. J. M. DE. *Sectarianism and Religious Persecution in China.* 2 vols. Amsterdam: J. Müller, 1903–4.

GRÜNWEDEL, ALBERT. *Buddhist Art in India.* Translated from the *Handbuch* of Professor Albert Grünwedel by Agnes C. Gibson; revised and enlarged by James Burgess. London: B. Quaritch, 1901.

HAAS, HANS. *Amida Buddha: Unsere Zuflucht, Urkunden zum Verständnis des japanischen Sukāvatī-Buddhismus.* Gottingen: Vandenhoeck, 1910.

HACKMANN, H. *Buddhism as a Religion: Its Historical Development and Its Present Conditions.* London: Probsthain, 1910.

HARA, KATSUHARA. *Introduction to the History of Japan.* New York: Putnam's, 1920.

HARDY, R. SPENCE. *Eastern Monachism.* London, 1850.

———. *Manual of Buddhism.* 1880.

HASTINGS, JAMES. *The Encyclopedia of Religion and Ethics.* New York: Scribners, 1908.

HEROLD, A. FERDINAND. *The Life of Buddha according to the Legends of Ancient India.* Translated from the French by Paul C. Blum. New York: Boni, 1927.

HODOUS, LEWIS. *Buddhism and Buddhists in China.* New York: Macmillan, 1924.

HIUEN-TSIANG. *Buddhist Records of the Western World.* Translated from the Chinese by Samuel Beal. Boston, 1885.

HUME, ROBERT ERNEST. *The World's Living Religions.* New York, 1925.

Imperial Gazetteer of India. 25 vols. and atlas. Oxford: Clarendon Press, 1908–9.

I-TSING. *Record of the Buddhist Religion as Practised in India (A.D. 671–695).* Translated by J. Takakusu with a letter from F. Max Müller. Oxford, 1896.

JOHNSTON, REGINALD FLEMING. *Buddhist China.* London: J. Murray, 1913.

KEITH, A. BERRIEDALE. *Buddhist Philosophy in India and Ceylon.* Oxford: Clarendon Press, 1923.

KERN, (J.) H. C. *Manual of Indian Buddhism.* Strasburg, 1896.

KLEEN, TYRA DE. *Mudras: The Ritual Hand-Poses of the Buddha Priests and the Shiva Priests of Bali.* London: Paul, Trench, Trübner, New York: Dutton, 1924.

KNOX, GEORGE WILLIAM. *The Development of Religion in Japan.* New York: Putnam's; London: Knickerbocker Press, 1907.

KROM, N. J. *The Life of Buddha on the Stupa of Barabudur according to the Lalitavistara Text.* The Hague: Martinus Nijhoff, 1926.

LAW, BIMALA CHARAN. *The Life and Works of Buddhaghosa.* 1923.

LE COQ, ALBERT VON. *Chotscho.* Berlin: Reimer, 1913.

———. *Die buddhistische Spätantike in Mittelasien.* 5 vols. Berlin: Reimer, 1922–26.

LEVI, SYLVAIN. *Mahayana-sutralamkara by Asanga.* Sanskrit text and French translation. Paris: Librairie Honore Champion, 1907.

LLOYD, ARTHUR. *Shinran and His Work.* Tokyo: Kyo Bun Kwan, 1910.

———. *The Creed of Half Japan.* London, 1911.

MCGOVERN, WILLIAM MONTGOMERY. *An Introduction to Mahayana Buddhism, with Special Reference to Chinese and Japanese Phases.* London, 1922.

———. *A Manual of Buddhist Philosophy.* New York, 1923.

MAHAVAMSA. *The Great Chronicle of Ceylon.* Translated by Geiger in the "Pali Text Society Series." (An older translation by Turnour contains late additions.)

MELCHERS, BERND. *China: Der Tempelbau: Die Lochan von Ling-yän-si.* Hagen, 1921.

MITTON, G. E. *The Lost Cities of Ceylon.*

MONIER-WILLIAMS, MONIER. *Buddhism.* London, 1889.

MURDOCH, JAMES, and YAMAGATA, ISOH. *A History of Japan during the Century of Early Foreign Intercourse (1542–1651).* Kobe: Japan Chronicle, 1903.

NANJIO, BUNYIU. *A Short History of Twelve Japanese Buddhist Sects.* Tokyo: Bukkyo-sho-ei-yoku, shupan-sha, 1866.

———. *A Catalogue of the Chinese Translation of the Buddhist Tripitaka.* Oxford, 1883.

NARIMAN, G. K. *Literary History of Sanscrit Buddhism.* Bombay: Taraporevala, 1920.

NUKARIYA, KAITEN. *The Religion of the Samurai: A Study of Zen Philosophy and Discipline in China and Japan.* London: Luzac, 1913.

OLDENBERG, HERMANN. *Buddha; His Life, His Doctrine, His Order.* Translated from the German by William Hoey. London, 1882.

OLTRAMARE, PAUL. *L'histoire des idées théosophiques dans L'Inde,* Vol. II. Paris: Musée Guimet, 1923.

PELLIOT, PAUL. *Les grottes de Touen-Houang.* 7 vols. Paris, 1920.

PERZYNSKI, FRIEDRICH. *Von Chinas Göttern.* München, 1920.

PRATT, JAMES BISSETT. *The Pilgrimage of Buddhism.* New York: Macmillan, 1928.

PRZYLUSKI, JEAN. *Le concile de Rājagṛha: Introduction à l'histoire du canon et des sectes bouddhiques.* Paris: Geuthner, 1926.

RADHAKRISHNAN, S. *Indian Philosophy.* 2 vols. London, 1923–27.

REICHELT, KARL L. *Truth and Tradition in Chinese Buddhism: A Study of Chinese Mahayana Buddhism.* Shanghai: Commercial Press, 1927.

REISCHAUER, A. K. *A Catechism of the Shin Sect.* 1912.

———. *Studies in Japanese Buddhism.* New York: Revell, 1917.

RICHARD, TIMOTHY. *New Testament of Higher Buddhism.* Edinburgh, 1910.

———. *The Awakening of Faith in the Mahayana Doctrine.* 2d ed. Shanghai, 1918.

ROSENBERG, DR. OTTO. *Die Probleme der buddhistischen Philosophie.* Heidelberg, 1924.

"Sacred Books of the East":

Sutta Nipata, Vol. X.

Vinaya Texts, Vols. XIII, XVII, XX.

Saddharma-Pundarika, Vol. XXI.

Buddha-Carita, Vol. XLIX.

Mahayana Texts, Vol. XLIX.

SANTI-DEVA. *Sikshā-samuccaya: A Compendium of Buddhist Doctrine.* Translated from the Sanskrit by Cecil Bendall and W. H. D. Rouse. London: J. Murray, 1922.

SATOMI, KISHIO. *Japanese Civilization.* 1924.

SAUNDERS, KENNETH J. *The Story of Buddhism.* Oxford, 1916.

———. *Gotama Buddha: A Biography.* (Based on the canonical books of the Theravadin). New York, 1920.

———. *Epochs of Buddhist History.* Chicago: University of Chicago Press, 1922.

———. *Buddhism and Buddhists in Southern Asia.* New York: Macmillan, 1923.

SHAKU, SOYEN. *Sermons of a Buddhist Abbott.* Chicago: Open Court, 1906.

SMITH, VINCENT ARTHUR. *Early History of India, Including Alexander's Campaigns.* Oxford, 1908.

———. *Asoka, the Buddhist Emperor of India.* Oxford, 1909.

———. *A History of Fine Art in India and Ceylon from the Earliest Times to the Present Day.* Oxford, 1911.

———. *Oxford Student's History of India.* 1915.

SŌGEN, YAMAKAMI. *Systems of Buddhistic Thought.* University of Calcutta, 1912.

STEIN, SIR MARK AUREL. *Sand-buried Ruins of Khotan: A Personal Narrative of a Journey of Archaeological Exploration in Chinese Turkestan.* London, 1903.

———. *Ancient Khotan: Detailed Report of Archaeological Explorations in Chinese Turkestan.* Oxford, 1907.

———. *Ruins of Desert Cathay: A Personal Narrative of Explorations in Central Asia and Westernmost China.* London: Macmillan, 1912.

———. *The Thousand Buddhas.* 2 vols. London: B. Quaritch, Ltd., 1921.

———. *Serindia: Detailed Report of Explorations in Central Asia and Westernmost China.* 5 vols. Oxford: Clarendon Press, 1921.

SUZUKI, DAISETZ TEITARO. *A'svaghosa's Awakening of Faith in the Mahayana.* Chicago: Open Court, 1900.

———. *Outlines of Mahayana Buddhism.* Chicago: Open Court, 1908.

———. *Essays in Zen Buddhism.* London: Luzac, 1927.

———. *Studies in the Lankavatara Sutra.* London: Paul, Trench, Trübner, 1930.

TARANATHA. *Geschichte des Buddhismus in Indien.* Translated from the Tibetan by Anton Schiefner. St. Petersburg, 1869.

THOMAS, EDWARD J. *The Life of Buddha as Legend and History.* New York: Knopf, 1927.

TOKIWA, DAIJO. *Buddhist Monuments in China.* 1926.

Transactions of the Third International Congress for the History of Religion. 2 vols. Oxford: Clarendon Press, 1908.

VALLÉE-POUSSIN, LOUIS DE LA. *Bouddhisme: Opinions sur l'histoire de la dogmatique: Leçons faites à l'institut.* Paris: Beauchesne, 1909.

———. *The Way to Nirvana.* Cambridge: University Press, 1917.

VISSER, M. W. DE. *The Arhats in China and Japan.* Berlin: Oesterheld, 1923.

WADDELL, L. AUSTIN. *The Buddhism of Tibet.* London, 1895.

WALLESER, M. "The Life of Nagarjuna: From Tibetan and Chinese Sources," *Hirth Anniversary Volume.* London: Probsthain, 1923.

WARREN, HENRY CLARKE. *Buddhism in Translations.* Harvard University Press, 1922.

WATTERS, THOMAS. *On Yuan Chwang's Travels in India.* London: Oriental Translation Fund, N.S., 1904–5.

WIEGER, LEON. *Bouddhisme chinois: Extraits du Tripitaka, des commentaires, tracts, etc.* 2 vols. Ho-kien-fou: Roman Catholic Press, 1910–13.

———. *Histoire des croyances religieuses et des opinions philosophiques en Chine, depuis l'origine, jusqu'à nos jours.* Ho-kien-fou, 1917. (Eng. trans., 1927; same pub.)

PERIODICAL ARTICLES CITED

Buddhist Annual of Ceylon. W. E. Bastian, "Colombo." (General reference.)

DHARMAPALA, ANAGARIKA. "On the Eightfold Path," *Asia,* September, 1927.

FRANKE, R. O. "The Buddhist Councils at Rajagaha and Vesali," *Journal of the Pali Text Society,* 1908.

HARAPRASADA, SASTRI. "Buddhism in Bengal since the Muhammadan Conquest," *Journal of the Asiatic Society of Bengal*, 1886.

LEVI, SYLVAIN. "Asvaghosha le Sutralankara et ses sources," *Journal asiatique*, XII (1908), 10, 77 ff.

LLOYD, ARTHUR. "Developments of Japanese Buddhism," *Transactions of Asiatic Society of Japan*, XXII (1884), 361–405.

MILLICAN, FRANK R. "T'ai Hsü and Modern Buddhism," *Chinese Recorder*, 1923, pp. 326–32.

———. "Buddhism in the Light of Modern Thought as Interpreted by the Monk T'ai Hsü," *ibid.*, 1926, pp. 91–94.

MINO, KOGETSU. "Shinran Revival of the Last Year," *Eastern Buddhist*, II, (1922), 285–91.

PERI, N. "Apropos de la date de Vasubandhu," *Bulletin de l'Ecole Française d'Extrême-Orient*, Vol. XI (1911).

SEIREN (BLUE LOTUS). "In Buddhist Temples." Four articles in the *Eastern Buddhist*, Vol. II (1922).

SUBRAHMANYA, AIYAR K. V. "Origin and Decline of Buddhism and Jainism in Southern India," *Indian Antiquary*, 1911.

SUZUKI, DAISETZ TEITARO. "The Revelation of New Truth in Zen Buddhism," *Eastern Buddhist*, I (1921), 194–228.

TAKAKUSU, J. *Life of Vasubandhu by Paramartha*. Translated in *T'oung Pao*, 1904, pp. 269 ff.

———. "A Study of Paramartha's Life of Vasubandhu and the Date of Vasubandhu," *Journal of the Royal Asiatic Society*, January, 1905.

TSU, YU YUE. "Present Tendencies in Chinese Buddhism," *Journal of Religion*, 1921, pp. 497–512.

———. "Diary of a Chinese Buddhist Nun, T'ze Kuang," *ibid.*, October, 1927, pp. 612–18.

VALLÉE-POUSSIN, L. DE LA. "Les counciles bouddhiques," *Museon*, 1905.

WATTERS, T. "The Eighteen Lohan of Chinese Buddhism," *Journal of the Royal Asiatic Society*, April, 1899.